Cromosys Publication

Teach Yourself Adobe Premiere Pro

NIRANJAN JHA SHOWMAN

Founder - Niranjan Jha Showman

Corporation

Education and Technology Research Center

Patankar Park, Nallasopara (W), Mumbai. +91-9561450045

Education, Technology, Publication, Healthcare, Newsmedia, Realtor, Filmmaking

www.facebook.com/cromosys

+91-9561450045
Learn Advanced Skills
And Get Job Instantly
GERMAN
Python
FRENCH
C++
SPANISH
Java
ENGLISH
HTML5
RUSSIAN
CSS
JavaScript
Cromosys
Education and Technology Research Center
Nallasopara (W), Mumbai

Learn Web Programming
Demo-Class Free
HTML
CSS
React
JavaScript
Typescript
Bootstrap
Cromosys
20 Years of Experience
Nallasopara (W), Mumbai
+91-9561450045

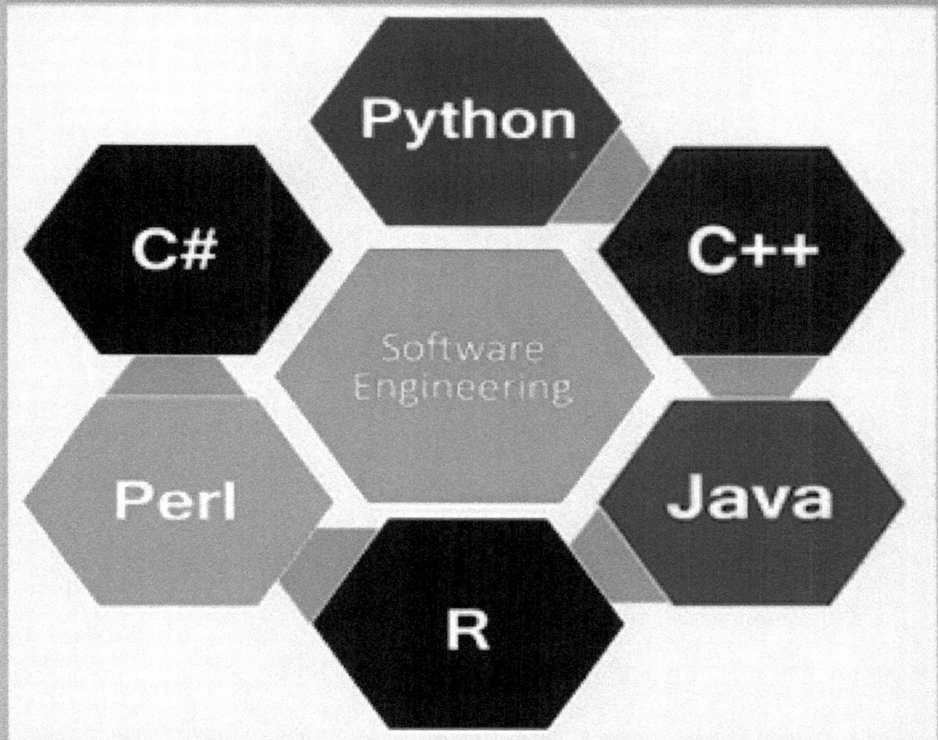

+91-9561450045
Learn Software Engineering
Demo-Class Free
Python
C#
C++
Software
Engineering
Perl
Java
R
Cromosys
20 Years of Experience
Nallasopara (W), Mumbai
+91-9561450045

25 Years of Experience
Learn Visual Multimedia
Animation VFX
Movie Editing
Game Development
Cromosys
+91-9561450045
Education and Technology Research Center
Nallasopara (W), Mumbai
www.facebook.com/cromosys

Jobs Available
For Candidates Who Know

German
French
Spanish

Vacancy in Germany, France, Spain

For Hospitality, Engineering, IT Sector

With Free Visa, Airfare and Accommodation

Cromosys
Education and Technology Research Centre
Nallasopara (W), Mumbai
+91-9561450045
20 Years of Experience

+91-9561450045
Foreign Languages Institute
German, French, Spanish
Basic and Advanced - All Levels
3 x 6 = 18 Courses
FRANCHISE
Business Offer
Teaching Materials Provided
We have 1 Million Students Globally
Great Income Assured
Global Exposure
Cromosys
20 Years of Experience
Nallasopara (W), Mumbai
+91-9561450045

Book: Teach Yourself Adobe Premiere Pro
Author: Niranjan Jha Showman
Publisher: Cromosys Publication
ISBN: Acquired
Date: 2020
Category: Computer Education

Preface

Cromosys Publication's **Teach Yourself Adobe Premiere Pro** book is an optimal quality guide to the beginners and advanced learners. We are the leading book publisher of languages and technology. Our research and education center working for last fifteen years has made tremendous efforts to simplify the learning of Premiere Pro, and so we assure you that this book will walk you through in the simplest way in your entire course of learning, and will make you a master of this application in just one month of time. This book introduces you to the world of video editing and lets you modify the video depending on your requirements. Using Adobe Premiere Pro, you can create videos for any occasions, ranging from simple presentations to complex programs or events. The content in this book is presented in such a way that it can be beneficial to both beginners as well as professionals. This all-inclusive book provides you with in-depth knowledge of various concepts, such as the user-interface and procedure to apply effects and transitions. An easy-to-understand, step-by-step approach, supplemented with practical implementation and many real-life screenshots are some of the distinguishing features of the book. In the tutorials of this book, you learn the procedure to create and modify a project, add audio and video effects and transitions, work with keyframes in animation, create titles and their utility, and render as well as export a final project. You also learn the new and improved features of Premiere Pro CS6 and the latest versions. The lessons conceived and prepared by us will help you start learning from real basic making your move amazing, astonishing, and exhilarating for you. It's cool, simple, and sublime!

Niranjan Showman, the author of this and fifty other books published online, is the coiner, founder, and owner of Cromosys Corporation. His dedication in technological and linguistic research is significantly known to millions of people around the world. This book is the creation of his avowed determination to make the learning of Premiere Pro easy to the people. After you install the application on your system, you just have to follow the instructions of this book doing the same on your computer, and you will see that you are quickly learning everything. Just an hour of practice per day, and in a month of time you'll get a lot of knowledge, tips and tricks to work with this software. This is an unmatchable unique book of its kind that guarantees your success. The lessons are magnificently powerful to bring you into the arena of cinematic video editing. With the industrial growth from the year 2014, the accurate and profound knowledge of this software has influenced millions of minds; therefore we conceived the idea of making this book a guideline to those who want to be perfect in this application starting from real basic. The Premiere Pro software enables you to perform various functions, such as editing a video, capturing a video from external devices such as camcorder or microphones, and create titles, special effects, or transitions. In addition, you can also output files into various formats. In this book, you begin with exploring new features available in Premiere Pro CS6. Later, you explore non-linear editing and about the system requirements, and then you learn to launch the application and create a project. You also learn to explore the user interface and get acquainted with the workspace. What Premiere Pro does, no other software can do. This all-inclusive book teaches you everything about Premiere Pro CS6 as it is easy, effective, and reliable. The quick and precise lessons with screenshots will help you enhance your creativity of crafting sophisticated high-quality digital video. It is the need of time and that is why many people have been sharpening their knowledge to be good in it.

Premiere Pro is an industry-standard application used for compositing. It is primarily used in the post production stage of film and television production. It is closely integrated with After Effects, Photoshop, and Illustrator to deliver superior quality motion graphics. Using Premiere Pro, you can manipulate and compose different media types including images, text, video, and audio. You will find various built-in tools or third party plug-ins with which you can enhance a video and create professional effects.

Cromosys, our education and technology research center, saving human efforts from being wasted, is committed to help you gain profound and contemporary knowledge. The world growing with density has brought enormous opportunity to video-editing talents irrespective of their geographical boundaries. We strongly believe that this book is useful for people working for motion pictures editing, graphics and animation, media houses, and entertainment world. After you start the lesson, you don't need to worry about anything but just follow each and every step carefully. This book is designed to fulfill the instant need of learners in a very economical way, as it is easy to find on Internet and affordable to buy and share. Cromosys, our path-breaking pioneer training institute for Computer Courses, English Speaking, Foreign Languages, and Competition Coaching, is dedicated to enlightening human mind with educational endeavors, and we are doing the same for last successful fifteen years. And recently we have come up with 'Worldwide Online Teaching System' for languages and technology. We not only hope but believe that your success is in your hand, as this book will take you miles ahead in your expectation. We always respect the views and comments of readers, so for any communication with regards to assistance, enquiry or collaboration, we are always there at your reach as it helps us improve our quality.

Niranjan Jha Showman
Founder: Cromosys Corporation
Web: facebook.com/cromosys
Contact no.   +91-9561450045
Email address: cromosys@yahoo.com
Nallasopara (W), Mumbai, India

Books by the same author:
Teach Yourself Adobe After Effects, Teach Yourself Adobe Flash, Teach Yourself Adobe Dreamweaver, Teach Yourself Autodesk Maya, Teach Yourself Autodesk Combustion, Teach Yourself Autodesk 3ds Max, English Voice Accent and Pronunciation, English Word Power, English Dictionary of Modern Slang, Teach Yourself Spanish, Teach Yourself French, Teach Yourself German

Cromosys
Education and Technology Research Center
Education, Technology, Publication, Healthcare, Realtor, Filmmaking
Nallasopara (W), Mumbai, India

Caution: All the writing works that include all the educational, non-educational books, novels, and articles of the author Niranjan Jha, are the registered contents of Online Digital Services and also published contents of his registered magazine FACE OFF - Inventing Truth, which carries registration no. MAHENG12112/13/1/2009-TC and the endorsement no. 3244 28/5/2009 with the Ministry of Information and Broadcasting, Govt. of India. Any plagiarism in this regard will attract strict legal action. Any further publication of any of his books requires his written permission. Copyright certificate of this book is attached at the end of this book.

Lesson 1
Introduction
Premiere Pro is an application that allows you to combine various media files, such as still images, image sequence, audio, and video to make a final required video. You can work with different tools to import, organize, edit, and preview almost any type of digital media. Whether you are a novice user or a professional, Premiere Pro enhances your creativity by crafting a sophisticated high-quality digital video. Adobe Premiere Pro is the efficient and precise video editing tool that helps you to create a perfect video along with over comings faced during the editorial, production, and workflow phases. This application allows you to work in a custom and task-oriented environment using a workspace, and you can customize the default workspace as required. In this chapter, you begin with exploring new features available in Premiere Pro CS6. Later, you explore non-linear editing and about the system requirements, if you wish to work on the Premiere Pro CS6 software. Further, you learn how to launch the application and create a project. Then, you explore the Premiere Pro user interface and get acquainted with the workspace.

Exploring the new Features
Before moving ahead, you should know about the new features included in Premiere Pro CS6 which will help you understand this application. Let us discuss about some of the new features of Adobe Premiere Pro CS6:

- **Native 64-bit and GPU accelerated performance with Adobe Mercury Playback:** Allows you to edit High Definition videos (HD) as smooth as Standard Digital videos (SD). The inclusion of Mercury Playback Engine enables you to open projects faster, refine effects, and higher resolution sequences. You can also preview the results of the applied effects instantly.
- **Expanded native tapeless workflows:** Allows you to edit videos natively from devices, such as cameras, resulting in saving production time transcoding or rewrapping. Premiere Pro CS6, gains native support the numerous video formats, such as HD50, AVCAM, DPX, AVC-Intra and enhanced RED.
- **Script to screen workflow:** Allows you the collaboration of Adobe Story with scripts, resulting in capturing of the key production. In other words, shot lists from the scripts are created automatically using Adobe OnLocation.
- **Editing and production efficiencies from metadata features:** Enables you to convert the speech dialogues into text with high accuracy. In addition to the conversion, you can also synchronize the content using Adobe Story script.
- **CS Review:** Refers to the online service that makes the reviews of client and the team simple, allowing you to share information easily everyday. The CS review feature eliminates the need of swapping of files and burning discs. Moreover, you can add comments to the video using a Web browser.
- **Streamlined encoding:** Allows you to distribute the content in any format as required using Adobe Media Encoder. This helps you to save time by performing batch encoding in various formats of the sequences present in a video.
- **Native support for DSLR cameras:** Enables you to edit a video from the Digital Single-Lens Reflex (DSLR) cameras. Inclusion of native support for these devices helps you to save production time transcoding or rewrapping.
- **Ultra key:** Helps you to easily perform the keying tasks. Let us now learn about non-linear editing.

Introducing Non-Linear Editing in Premiere Pro CS6

Earlier, the only method to edit videos was linear (tape-to-tape) editing. Gradually, the non-linear method was evolved, during the 1990s. In the beginning, non-linear editing faced several oppositions from the video editors, but gradually, it was accepted for those advantages it provides, such as script to screen workflows. Adobe Premiere Pro is a non-linear editor that can edit a video efficiently. Using Premiere Pro, you can randomly access, that is non-sequentially, any frame of the imported video clip and perform functions such as replace and trim. In addition, you can also move clips anywhere you want in the final video. Non-linear editing allows you to ease the editing process by simply dragging clips and segments of the video to the desired position in the final video. Apart from this, one of the advantages is that you have direct access to the source video clip. In other words, you do not have to forward or rewind the video tape, as in case of linear editing.

Understanding the System Requirements

There are certain system requirements that you need to understand before you install the application on a computer. Premiere Pro CS6 is now 64-bit native that enables you to use full memory of the CPU, when users are working on high-resolution projects. You need to verify that your computer is equipped with the essential system requirements to install and use Premiere Pro CS6. The system requirements include both software (primarily the operating system and the Web browsers) and hardware of the computer. Following are the minimum system requirements for Premiere Pro CS6, Windows operating system:

- Intel Core 2 Duo or AMD Phenom II processor (64-bit support required)
- 64-bit operating system required: Microsoft Vista or Windows 7
- 2 Giga Byte (GB) of Random Access Memory [RAM] (4 GB recommended)
- 12 GB of available hard disk space plus additional free space required during installation (cannot install on removable flash storage devices)
- 7200 rpm (revolution per minute) hard drive to edit compressed video formats (Redundant Arrays of Inexpensive Disks (RAID) 0 for uncompressed)
- 1280x900 display with OpenGL 2.0 compatible graphics card (OpenGL is a set of standards used for high-performance 2D and 3D graphics)
- Adobe-certified Graphics Processing Unit (GPU) card for GPU accelerated computer system performance
- Adobe-certified card for capture and export to tape for Standard Definition (SD)/High Definition (HD) workflows
- OHCI-compatible IEEE 1394 port for Digital Video (DV)/High Digital Video (HDV) capture, export to tape, and transmit to DV devices
- Sound card compatible with Audio Stream Input/Output (ASIO) protocol or Microsoft Windows Driver Model
- DVD-ROM drive
- QuickTime 7.6.2 software required for QuickTime features
- Adobe Flash Player 10 software required to play back DVD projects that are exported as Shockwave Flash (SWF) files
- Broadband Internet connection required for online services. Let's now learn to launch the Premiere Pro CS6 application.

Launching Premiere Pro CS6

Before you start editing any video in Premiere Pro CS6, you need to start the application. Perform the following steps to launch Premiere Pro CS6:

1. Click the **Start** button on your desktop, and select **All Programs** option in the Start menu. A list of all the programs installed in the system appears.

2. Select **Adobe Master Collection CS6** and choose **Adobe Premiere Pro CS6** from the list. The Adobe Premiere Pro CS6 splash screen appears. The welcome screen of Adobe Premiere Pro CS6 application appears, as shown in picture 1.1.

Picture 1.1

Creating a New Project

After you launch Adobe Premiere Pro CS6, the application opens the welcome screen, which provides direct options to work with a video. However, you can perform the same tasks using the options available in the Menu bar. For example, you can use the options available in the File menu to create a new document or open a recent document. Premiere Pro also provides a separate project panel in the user interface (UI) for every project that is created. A project in Premiere Pro is referred to as a collection consisting of sequences and assets, such as transitions and effects. For any project, Premiere Pro creates a project file that consists of all the settings and data related to the sequences and assets. Note that the project file does not store any video, audio, or image objects; it only contains the references for these objects. These objects are referred to as clips and based on the name and location of a clip file during its import.

In addition to the clip references, a project can include multiple sequences. A sequence can either be an individual video or an audio clip in itself or a part of the whole project. Multiple sequences combined together can result in a complete video, which is edited depending on the requirement. Now perform the following steps to create a new project in Premiere Pro CS6:

1. Click the **New Project** button on the welcome screen of Premiere Pro CS6. It opens the New Project dialog box.

2. Click the **Browse** button at the bottom to specify the location where you want the project to be saved on your system. It opens the Browse For folder dialog box on the screen.

3. **Select** the desired folder where you want to save the project. In our case, we select the Projects folder.

4. Click the **OK** button on the dialog box. The desired location is specified in the **Location** dropdown in the New Project dialog box.

5. **Type** the name of the project in the Name text box. In our case, we type: **Sample_proj1** as the project name. Then click the **OK** button. A new project is created and the New Sequence dialog box appears, as shown in picture 1.2.

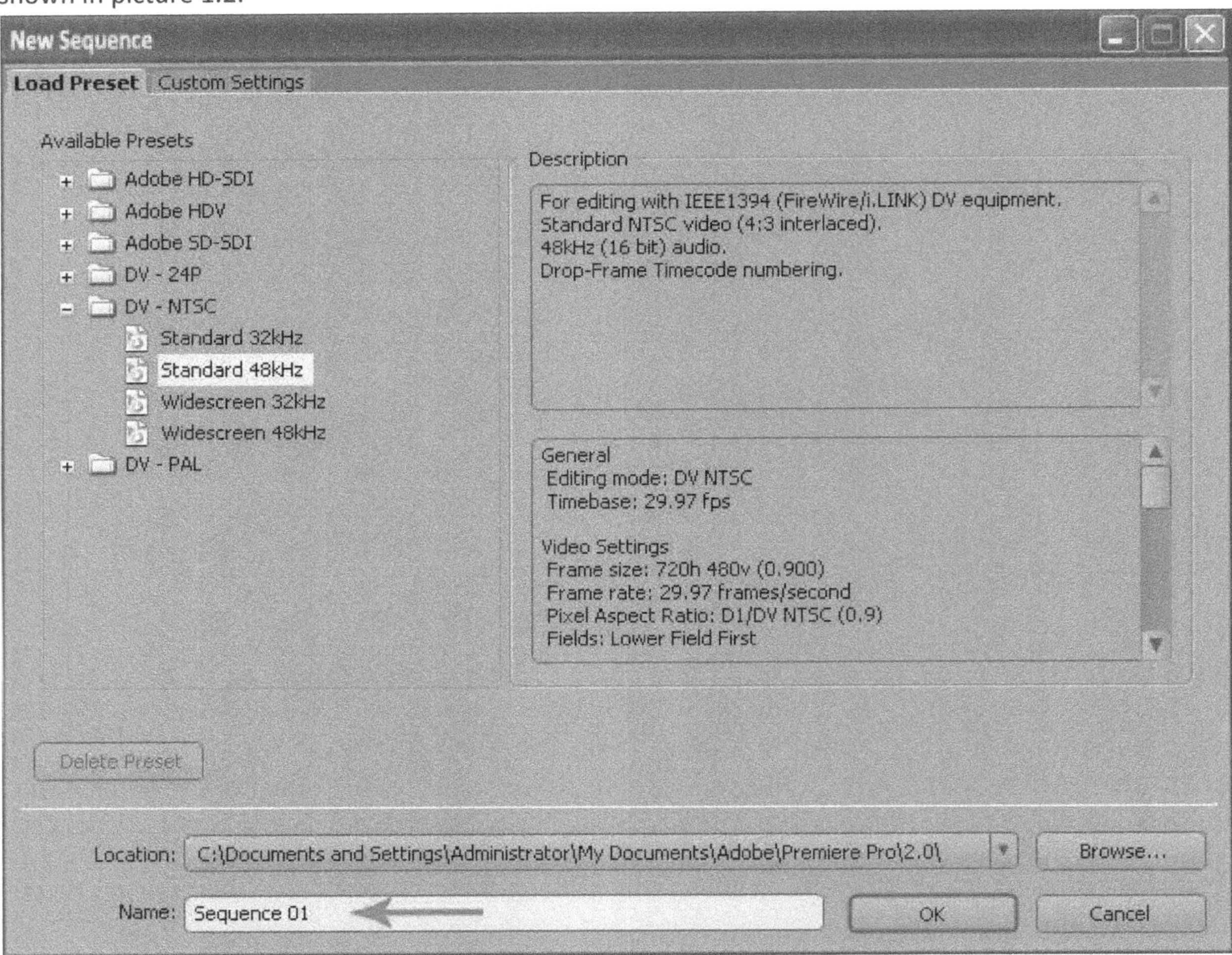

Picture 1.2

6. **Type** the name of the sequence in the Sequence Name text box. In our case, we type the sequence with the default name: **Sequence 01**. Then click the **OK** button at the bottom.

A project with a sequence is created and the User Interface (UI) of the Premiere Pro CS6 appears, as shown in picture 1.3. In this picture, the red arrow numbered 1 shows the **Title bar**, arrow numbered 2: **Menu bar**, 3: **Tools panel**, 4: **Project panel**, 5: **Source Monitor panel**, 6: **Effect Controls panel**, 7: **Audio Mixer panel**, 8: **Program Monitor panel**, 9: **Info panel**, 10: **History panel**, 11: **Effects panel**, 12: **Timeline panel**, 13: **Audio Master Meters**. You will learn about all these panels in the following lesson.

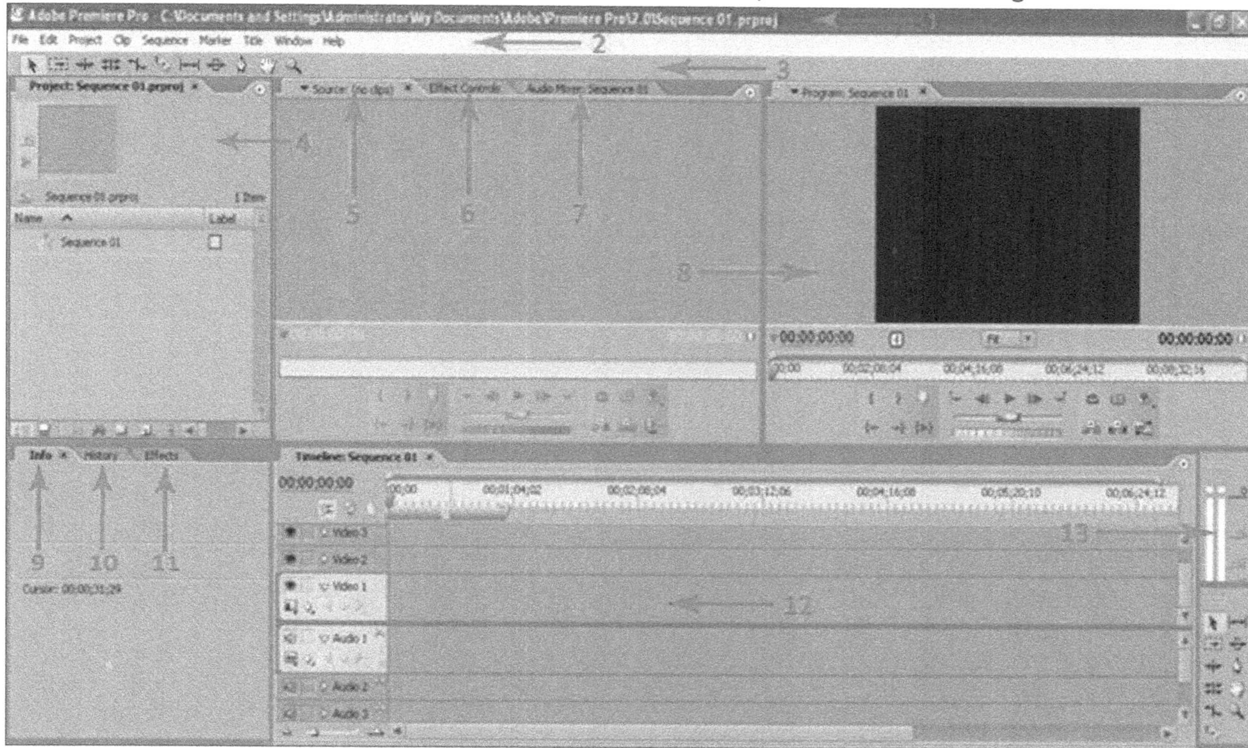

Picture 1.3

Selecting Project Settings

Premiere Pro allows you to customize the project settings depending on the requirement. With separate dialog box for each project, sequence, and preferences, you can easily customize the parameters and options under a specific category. In this section, you get familiar with the following dialog boxes: (1) Project Settings, (2) Sequence Settings, and (3) Preferences.

Specifying Project Settings

You can set the required settings for any project either at the time of its creation or by selecting the Project> Project Settings from the Menu bar. The Project Settings dialog box consists of two tabs, namely <u>General</u> and <u>Scratch Disks</u>. Let us have a brief description of these tabs. The General tab consists of the following options:

- **Title Safe Area**: Specifies the extent up to which the frame edge can be marked as a safe zone for titles to display complete titles on an output screen, such as television.
- **Action Safe Area**: Specifies the extent up to which the frame edge can be marked as a safe zone to display complete titles on an output screen, such as television set overscan.
- **Display Format (Video and Audio):** Allows you to display audio and video of various formats.
- **Capture Formats:** Allows you to capture video of various formats.

The Scratch Disks tab consists of the following options:
- **Captured Video:** Stores captured videos in the specified location. By default, the option Same as Project is selected.
- **Captured Audio:** Stores captured audio files in the specified location. By default, the option Same as Project is selected.
- **Video Previews:** Stores video preview files in the specified location. By default, the option Same as Project is selected.
- **Audio Previews:** Stores audio preview files in the specified location. By default, the option Same as Project is selected.

Specifying Sequence Settings

The Sequence Settings dialog box is used for the sequence settings in a video. It consists of various options broadly categorized as General, Video, Audio, and Video Previews. A brief description of these options is listed as follows:

- **Editing Mode:** Lets you set the video formats for preview files, timebase, compressive methods, and display formats
- **Timebase:** Specifies the time divisions that is required to calculate the position of time after every edit
- **Frame Size:** Allows you to specify the frame dimensions of the source in pixels
- **Pixel Aspect Ratio:** Lets you set the aspect ratio for individual pixels of analog video or images
- **Fields:** Enables you to specify the order for field of each frame
- **Display Format:** Allows you to display video in numerous timecode formats, such as film format
- **Preview File Format:** Allows you to select a file format that enables you to match previews in high quality, considering the rendering time and the file size of the video
- **Coder:** Allows you to specify the codec of preview files, such as UYUY 422 8-bit code SD-SDI
- **Width:** Allows you to specify the width of the frame used for previewing a video
- **Height:** Allows you to specify the height of the frame used for previewing a video
- **Reset:** Sets all the parameters to their default settings
- **Maximum Bit Depth:** Allows you to set maximum bit depth of color, up to 32bpc
- **Maximum Render Quality:** Maximizes the quality of motion produced when the clips and sequences are rendered

Setting Preferences

Using the Preferences dialog box in Premiere Pro, you can change the look and appearance of this application as required. You can customize the options present under the categories; General, Appearance, Audio, Audio Hardware, Audio Output Mapping, Auto Save, Capture, Device Control, Label Colors, Label Defaults, Media, Memory, Player Settings, Titler, Trim. A brief description of these categories is as follows:

- **General:** Allows you to set the time for options, such as Preroll, Postroll, Video Transition Default Duration, Audio Transition Default Duration, and Still Image Default Duration. In addition, you can also set the audio track and bin settings using those options present under the General category.

- **Appearance:** Enables you to set the brightness of the user interface.
- **Audio:** Allows you to adjust the Adjust the Automatch Time parameters, such as Pan and Effect, and allows you to specify how source channels are mixed to 5.1 audio tracks.
- **Audio Hardware:** Allows specifying the audio hardware device and its corresponding settings.
- **Audio output Mapping:** Maps the specified speaker with its supported audio channel.
- **Auto Save:** Allows you to set time duration and versions to save the projects automatically.
- **Capture:** Enables you to customize the settings, in case a video or an audio is captured directly from camera.
- **Device Control:** Allows you to select a playback/recording device and set its properties, such as Preroll and Timecode Offset.
- **Label Colors:** Allows you to customize the color and its name for the label assets.
- **Label Defaults:** Allows you to set the default label colors to the assets, such as bins, sequence, or video.
- **Media:** Allows setting the preferences for inserted media, such as Framecode and Timecount.
- **Memory:** Specifies the amount of RAM available for Premiere Pro and software supported by it.
- **Player Settings:** Allows you to set the player, where the edited videos will be played.
- **Titler:** Allows you to change the letter style present in the Titler Style Swatches panel and the Font Browser.
- **Trim:** Allows you to se the trim point, earlier or later, from the desired frame.

Lesson 2
User Interface and Workspace

Premiere Pro CS6 offers a wide range of features and tools to help you in various ways, such as to view the source and the edited video clip, to work with the sequences, and to view the information related to the particular asset imported in a clip. These features and tools are available in the form of user interface elements, making it comprehensive and extensive. Due to elaborate and all-encompassing design of the user interface, you may initially face some difficulties in finding a particular feature or tool. Therefore, it is essential to be familiar with the main elements present in the user interface, as already shown in picture 1.3. The user interface consists of the following elements: Title bar, Menu bar, Tools panel, Project panel, Resource Central panel, Source Monitor panel, Effects Controls panel, Audio Mixer panel, Program Monitor panel, Media Browser panel, Info panel, Effects panel, History panel, Sequence, Tracks, Timeline panel, Clips, and Audio Master Meters.

Exploring the Title bar

This is the topmost bar in the user interface that displays the name of application and the full path where the currently opened project is saved. This bar is shown in picture 1.3 with the red arrow numbered 1. In addition, the title bar also consists of the window controls; Minimize, Maximize/Restore, and Close buttons on the top right corners.

Exploring the Menu bar

The Menu bar is located just below the Title bar and provides you with various options, present under different menus, such as File, Edit, Project, Clip, Sequence, Marker, Title, Window, and Help. This bar is shown in picture 1.3 with the red arrow numbered 2.

Exploring the Tools Panel

The Tools panel provides icons of the commonly used tools, such as Selection, Slip, and Razor tool. This panel is shown in picture 1.3 with the red arrow numbered 3. A brief description of these tools is as follows:

- **Selection Tool:** Lets you select various objects, such as clips and menu items
- **Track Select Tool:** Lets you select all the clips in a sequence that are present to the right of the cursor
- **Ripple Edit Tool:** Lets you trim the In and Out point of a clip in the Timeline panel. This tool also deletes the gap caused due to editing
- **Rolling Edit Tool:** Lets you roll the point of edit between two clips in the Timeline panel
- **Rate Stretch Tool:** Lets you reduce the playing time of the clip by making its playback time speedier
- **Razor Tool:** Allows you to make incisions among the clips placed in the Timeline panel in order to apply transitions
- **Slip Tool:** Allows you to work simultaneously with the In and Out points of a clip taking into consideration the time span between the original and the edited clip
- **Slide Tool:** Moves the required clip to the desired position in the Timeline panel
- **Pen Tool:** Allows you to select and set the keyframes and adjust the connector lines in the Timeline panel
- **Hand Tool:** Enables you to move the Timeline viewing area
- **Zoom Tool:** Lets you to zoom in and zoom out the size of the viewing area of the Timeline panel

Exploring the Project Panel

In the Project panel, you can place all the assets, such as clips or images, required to edit a video. Using bins and folders you can organize these assets for easy navigation. The picture 1.3 with the red arrow numbered 4 shows the Project panel.

Exploring the Source Monitor Panel

The Source Monitor panel refers to the screen where you can view the original clips and trim it according to the requirement. This panel is shown in picture 1.3 with the red arrow numbered 5.

Exploring the Effect Controls Panel

The Effect Controls panel allows you to change the effects of the clip selected in the Timeline panel, such as Motion Opacity. By default, for a selected clip, there are three video effects; Motion, Opacity, and Time Remapping, whereas, an audio clip has only one default effect that is Volume. The picture 1.3 with the red arrow numbered 6 indicates the Effect Controls panel.

Exploring the Audio Mixer Panel

Using the Audio Mixer panel, you can adjust different audio tracks while listening to them. You can also set the advanced audio settings, such as volume and pan/balance. The picture 1.3 with the red arrow numbered 7 indicates this option tab. When you click the tab, it opens the Audio Mixer panel as shown in picture 1.4 below.

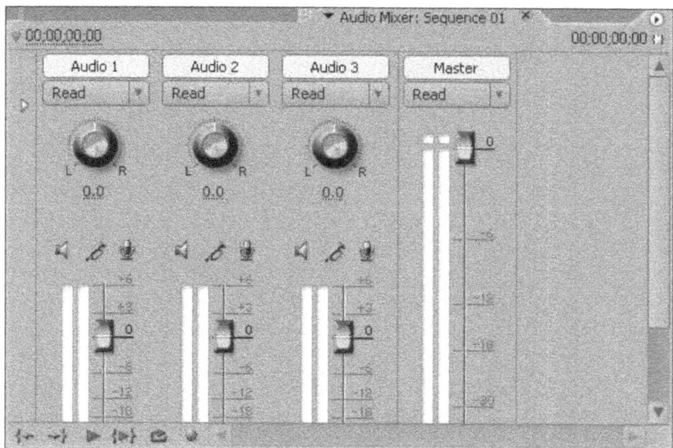

Picture 1.4

Exploring the Program Monitor Panel

The Program Monitor panel lets you view the edited clip or in other words, preview of a clip which is in progress. The picture 1.3 with the red arrow numbered 8 shows the Program Monitor panel.

Exploring the Info Panel

The Info panel (picture 1.3 with the red arrow numbered 9) provides you with the metadata of the clip selected in the Timeline panel.

Exploring the History Panel

The History panel (picture 1.3 with the red arrow numbered 10) provides you with history of the actions performed during the production of the video. It keeps track of last 32 steps or the actions you have performed.

Exploring the Effects Panel

Using the Effects panel, (picture 1.3 with the red arrow numbered 11) you can apply numerous effects and transitions to the assets and clips in the Timeline panel.

Exploring the Timeline Panel

The Timeline panel (picture 1.3 with the red arrow numbered 12) allows you to either break up a clip into manageable parts or to combine multiple clip parts into a single clip. It also represents the duration of any clip or asset in a horizontal bar. This type of time representation helps you to zoom in or zoom out the clips. The Timeline panel consists of Sequences, Tracks, and Clips. A brief description of these is as follows:

- **Sequence:** Acts as a container of a project created in Premiere Pro where all the clips are placed
- **Tracks:** Refers to the layers where multiple audio and video clips can be placed separately
- **Clips:** Refers to the assets, such as imported audio and video

Exploring the Audio Master Meters
Using the Audio Master Meters (picture 1.3 with the red arrow numbered 13), the overall audio of the master track present in the Timeline panel can be played.

Working with Workspace
You can work in a custom and task-oriented environment using a workspace in Premiere Pro. A workspace is a collection of menus, toolbars, palettes, and Ribbon control panels. This workspace switching feature ensures the production output for professional designers. When you perform a task using a workspace, only those menus, toolbars, palettes and options in Ribbon relevant to the workspace are displayed. You can also customize the workspace and save it with a user-defined name. In the following section, you learn to customize and save the workspace.

Customizing the Workspace
Premiere Pro allows you to customize its default workspace as required, such as one workspace is created for editing purpose and another for previewing the edited video. You can customize the workspace by changing the size of the required panel or frame; however, when you change the size of one panel, the size of its corresponding panel changes automatically. In addition, since the panels present in the Premiere Pro are dockable, you can easily drag them from one location to another. In our case, we are going to insert a panel and resize it. Perform the following steps to customize a workspace:

1. Select **Window> Multi-Camera Monitor** from the Menu bar. It opens the Multi-Camera window on the screen.

2. **Click** the gripper area (at the top-left corner) of the window that you want to move from one location to another. In our case, we select the gripper area of the Multi-Camera window.

3. **Drag** the Multi-Camera window to the desired location. You will see that the Multi-Camera window moves to that location.

4. **Click** the panel that you want to resize. In our case, we click the Audio Master Meters panel. Then **place** the mouse-pointer on the panel border. You will see that the shape of the mouse-pointer changes on the screen.

5. **Drag** the mouse-pointer to obtain the required panel size. Then **release** the mouse pointer. The Audio Master Meters panel is resized.

Saving a Workspace
After you have made all the changes in the workspace as required, you can save it for further use. When you made the changes, they are not saved automatically; as soon as you close the application window, the changes that you have made are lost. In order to retain those changes you need to save them. Perform the following steps to save a workspace:

1. Click the **Workspace** menu to open a dropdown list, as shown in picture 1.5. Then **select** the desired option. In our case, we select **New Workspace** option, which opens the New Workspace dialog box.

Picture 1.5

2. **Type** the desired name of the workspace in the <u>Name</u> text box. In our case, we type the name as: **My Workspace**.

3. Click the **OK** button. The modified workspace is saved with the specified name.

Closing a Project

After you have finished working with a project, you can close the project and quit the Premiere Pro application. Before you do that, you need to make sure that the currently opened project is saved in order to avoid loss of data. Perform the following steps to close the project:

1. Choose **File**> **Close Project** from the Menu bar of the Premiere Pro screen. The project is closed and the welcome screen appears.

2. Click the **Exit** button on the welcome screen to quit Premiere Pro. The Premiere Pro application closes.

Lesson 3
Working with Media

Premiere Pro allows you to combine various media files, such as still images, image sequence, audio, and video to make a final required video. You can work with different tools to import, organize, edit, and preview almost any type of digital media. Arranging all the assets appropriately is beneficial yet an important task. The concept of organizing various media files to facilitate easy access is known as media management. You can manage the media files on your hard drive and organize different media references that you import into Premiere Pro.

The first step in a new Premiere Pro project is to import various media files, which are to be used in editing a video. The Project panel provides several options to import and arrange all the assets (media files) of the project. There are icons that let you create new bins or items, views, or find the media files. You can also customize the Project panel as required. In this lesson, you get acquainted with the basic workflow of the video editing process. Next, in the lesson, you learn to import different files, such as still images and the image sequence. You also get to explore different file formats supported by Premiere Pro CS6 and learn to manage the imported files in the Project panel. In the end, you get to familiarize with the concept of aspect ratio.

Understanding the Basic Workflow

In this section, you learn about the basic procedure followed by non-linear editors, such as Premiere Pro. A sequential approach is followed in the traditional method of video editing. This sequential approach is as follows:

(A) The first step is to shoot the video.
(B) Next step is to capture the video to the hard drive of a computer. In other words, you need to transfer the video that you shoot to the hard drive.
(C) After the video is transferred or saved, you can import it to the Premiere Pro application.
(D) Edit the imported video as required, such as trimming the video or adding clips to the original video.
(E) After inserting the required clips, you can add text or create basic graphics to the edited video.
(F) You can also add an audio clip to the video to make it interactive. The audio can be anything, such as narration by a person about the video or background music to be played during the video.
(G) You can apply transitions, audio and video effects; mix multiple audio tracks in the edited video.
(H) After completing the video and the project as required, you can export this video to any media device, such as your computer, to a videotape, or a DVD.

Importing Media Files

In Adobe Premiere Pro, you can import numerous types of clips, such as multiple graphics, audios, videos, or still images to the original video to make it more attractive and alluring. Consider a scenario, where, you want to make a video from the images and add an audio to it. In that case, you can import the images and audio separately in the Project panel and combine them to make the desired video. You can also add and mix multiple audio and video clips to the project. In this section, you can familiarize with the file formats supported by the Premiere Pro CS6. Next, you learn the procedure to import various media clips that includes still image, image sequence, audio, and video. You also learn to import these media clips using the Media Browser panel. Let's begin by exploring the file formats.

Exploring Supported File Formats

As already said in the preceding sections, the Premiere Pro CS6 supports a wide variety of file formats to import, such as MOV, AVI, or FLV. Some of the formats supported are listed below:

File formats supported by Premiere Pro CS6

File Types	File Extensions	Description
3GPP file format/3GPP2 file format	3GP/3G2	Refers to the Third Generation Partnership Project multimedia services that are mostly used on 3G phones; it can also be used on 2G and 4G phones
Audio Video Interleave	AVI	Acts as a container for both audio as well as video data and allows synchronized playback of audio with video
Digital Video	DV	Refers to the format used for recording and playback of the digital video
Flash Video	FLV	Allows you to play video files over the Internet using Adobe Flash Player
Graphics Interchange Format	GIF	Refers to the most commonly used format for bitmap images
QuickTime Movie	MOV	Refers to the file format of those videos played using QuickTime

Moving Pictures Expert Group	MPEG	Refers to the file format that derives its name from the group forming it and is used for compression and transmission of audio and video
Shockwave Flash Movie	SWF	Refers to the file format that is used for vector graphics, multimedia, and ActionScript in the Adobe Flash environment
Windows Media Video	WMV	Refers to video compression format
Advanced Audio Coding	AAC	Refers to the encoding scheme for digital audio
Audio Interchange File Format	AIFF	Allows you to store audio for personal use, such as on a computer
Windows Media Audio	WMA	Refers to the compression technology of the audio data
Waveform Audio Format	WAVE/WAV	Allows you to save bitstream of audios on computers
Bitmap Image File	BMP	Refers to the raster graphics image file format that is used to store bitmap digital files
Joint Photographic Experts Group	JPEG	Refers to one of the methods to save images. This format is best for images that resemble realistic scenes such as scenery
Portable Network Graphics	PNG	Enables you to save an image with the alpha channel. This format supports grayscale and palette based images
Photoshop Document	PSD	Refers to the native document format in Photoshop
Tagged Image File Format	TIFF	Refers to the most preferred image format because of its property of adaptability

Importing Still Image

As already discussed, Premiere Pro allows you to import still images to a project. You can place the imported images between different clips to provide smooth transition from one clip to another. Perform the following steps to import a still image in a project:

1. **Open** the project in which you want to import the still image. In our case, we open **Sample_proj1** on the screen.

2. Choose **File> Import** from the Menu bar to open the Import dialog box. Then **browse** to the location where the image is stored. In our case, we select the **Sample Pictures** folder.

3. **Select** the required image, and click the **Open** button. The Import Files dialog box appears showing the progress of the import process. This dialog box closes automatically after the file is imported in the Project panel.

Importing Image Sequences

Using Premiere Pro, you can also create a video from a group of the sequenced images. Consider a case, where you have created an animation using number of still images and you want to convert these sequenced images to a video. In such case, Premiere Pro allows you to import the group of image collectively. However, note that the images are arranged in a sequential order. Perform the following steps to import an image sequence:

1. **Open** the project in which you want to import the image sequence. In our case, we open the Sample_proj1 project.

2. Choose **File> Import** from the Menu bar to open the Import dialog box. Then **browse** to the folder where the images are stored. In our case, we select New Folder.

3. **Select** the first image sequence. Then **enable** (put check mark) Numbered Still checkbox which is at the bottom of the dialog box.

4. Click the **Open** button at the bottom. The Import Files dialog box appears showing the progress of the import process. As the result, the sequenced images are imported in the Project panel.

Importing Digital Audio/Video

Apart from still images and sequenced images, you can also import required audio and video clips stored in a computer. You can modify these imported clips as required; you can trim or reduce the playback time of these. The procedure to import a video or an audio is the same. Although, most of the videos consist of audio clips, you can delete them from the video, if required. Perform the following steps to import a video:

1. **Open** the project (Sample_proj1) in which you want to import the image sequence. Then choose **File> Import** from the Menu bar to open the Import dialog box.

2. **Browse** and **select** the required video, and click the **Open** button at the bottom of the dialog box. As the result, the selected video is imported in the Project panel.

Importing Media Clips Using Media Browser

Media Browser is a panel available on the left of Info panel and at the bottom-left of Premiere Pro CS6 screen. You can also import the required clips from the Media Browser panel, by performing the following steps:

1. **Click** to select the Media Browser panel which you find at the bottom-left of the Premiere Pro CS6 screen.

2. **Press** the Tilde (~) key on the keyboard to expand the Media Browser panel to full screen. Then **select** the required location to import the clips. In our case, we select D: (Local Disk) drive.

3. **Double-click** the clip that you want to import. As the result, the still image is imported in the Project panel.

Managing Media Files

The arrangement of media files is one of the important tasks. If all the assets and clips are properly arranged, you can save a lot of time from searching the required files. You can arrange the assets and access them using the Project panel. You can create bins and place the assets in them, customize the Project panel as required or based on the work with the bins. You can also label, rename, remove, and change the frame rate of media files. Let's begin by learning to customize the Project panel:

Customizing the Project Panel

Premiere Pro allows you to customize the Project panel as required. You can select a desired view, such as a list view or the icon view. You can also fix the size of the thumbnails and resize the frame as needed. Perform the following steps to customize the Project panel:

1. **Click** to select the Project panel, and **press** the Tilde (~) on the keyboard to maximize the Project panel.

2. **Click** the Project panel menu button (▶) which is at the top-right corner of Project panel. Then choose **View> Icon** from the list.

3. **Click** the same Project panel menu button (▶) which is at the top-right corner of Project panel. Then choose **Thumbnails> Off** to deselect it. As the result, the thumbnails appear on the screen.

4. **Press** the Tilde (~) key on the keyboard to minimize the Project panel. The Project panel is minimized to its default position.

Working with Bins

In Premiere Pro, the concept of bins is similar to the folder concept of windows. As in folders, you store all your assets at one location; you can use the bins for the same purpose. For example, you can create a parent bin for a project where all assets related to it are stored. You can also create multiple child bins as needed to separately store still images, audios, and videos. Perform these steps to work with a bin:

1. **Press** the Tilde key from the keyboard to maximize the Project panel. Then click the **New Bin** button to create a new bin. A new bin with the default name: Bin 01 is created.

2. **Select** the media files that you want to move to the bin. Then **drag** them to Bin 01. As the result, the selected files move to the specified bin.

3. **Double-click** the Bin 01 bin icon to open it. Bin 01 opens in a new window and consists of the files that you have moved in the preceding steps. Then click the **Close** button to close the bin window, and **press** the Tilde key from the keyboard to minimize the Project panel.

Working with Bins

In Premiere Pro, labels are color representations of the media files imported in the Project panel. By default, labels are assigned certain colors. However, you can customize these colors as required. Perform the following steps to change the color of a label:

1. **Press** the Tilde key from the keyboard to maximize the Project panel. Then **click** the Project panel menu button to open the dropdown list.

2. Choose **View> List** option to view the clips as a list. As the result, all the clips in the Project panel appear as a list.

3. **Select** the label by clicking the rectangular box that you want to modify. In our case, we select the label named: Sequence 01 project.

4. Choose **Edit> Label> Green** from the Menu bar. As the result the Green color is applied to the selected label.

Renaming Media Files

The media files are imported or created with their default name. However, you can rename them as required. It helps in easy navigation among various media files. Perform the following steps to rename a media file:

1. **Right-click** the media file that you want to rename. In our case, we right-click the bin media file to rename. It opens a context menu.

2. Select the **Rename** option, and **type** a name (Parent Bin) in the text box. Then press the **Enter** key to rename the bin as: Parent Bin.

Removing Media Files from a Project

At times, you may not require a particular media file in a project. In such a case, Premiere Pro allows you to delete that specific media file easily. Perform the following steps to remove a media file:

1. **Click** to select the media file in the Project panel that you want to delete. When you select, the media file gets highlighted.

2. Click the **Clear** button at the bottom-left side of the Project panel. As the result, the media file is deleted.

Changing the Frame Rate of Media Files

Using the Interpret Footage command in Premiere Pro, you can modify the frame rate for a clip as required. Whenever you change the frame rate for a clip, the playback duration of that clip also changes proportionally. Playback time for a clip refers to the time duration the clip is played. However, you can change this time duration and speed. Perform these steps to change the frame rate for a media file:

1. **Select** the media file whose frame rate you want to change. In our case, we select **Wildlife.wmv** media file.

2. Choose **Clip> Modify> Interpret Footage** from the Menu bar. It opens the Modify Clip dialog box on the screen.

3. **Select** the ratio button beside the **Assume this frame rate** option. Then **type** the required frame rate value in the fps text box. In our case, we type the value as: 25.

4. Click the **OK** button at the bottom. As the result, the frame rate of the required clip changes to **25.00** fps.

By default, in the Modify Clip dialog box, the radio button beside the Use Frame Rate from File option is selected and the value in the fps text box is 1.00.

5. **Press** the Tilde key from the keyboard to restore the Project panel to its default position. Let's now get acquainted with the aspect ratios.

Understanding the Aspect Ratio

An aspect ratio refers to the ratio of width to height and is of two types; frame aspect ratio and pixel aspect ratio. Frame aspect ratio defines the ratio for the frames of videos and still images. Pixel aspect ratio defines the ratio of the pixels that are required to make the frames. In Premiere Pro, the frame and pixel ratios are set during the project creation. You cannot modify it after creating the project. In this section, you get acquainted with:

- **Frame aspect ratio:** Refers to the ratio of width to height of a particular video or still image frame. The frame aspect can be of value 4:3 (width of 4.0 to height of 3.0) for a DV NTSC or 16:9 width of 16.0 to height of 9.0) for a commonly used widescreen camera.
- **Pixel aspect ratio:** Refers to the ratio of width to height of a single pixel in a frame. This aspect ratio varies greatly, as different video systems assume different number of pixels to fill a frame. For example, a frame aspect ratio of 4:3 refers to the ratio of 640 pixels wide by 480 pixels high.

Lesson 4
Previewing Media Files

Premiere Pro allows you to preview media files imported in the project anytime. You can preview any type of imported media clips, whether it is a still image, an image sequence, an audio, or a video helping in the video editing process. To preview the files, you can either double-click a file from the Project panel or drag the required clip from the Project panel to the Source Monitor panel. In this chapter, we discuss the dual panels, Source Monitor, and Program Monitor, present in Premiere Pro CS6. Next, you learn how to preview the media files, and how to trim the clip. You will also learn the procedure of looping the media files, audio as well as video.

Overview of Source and Program Monitor Panel

Premiere Pro provides you with dual panels, Source Monitor and Program Monitor. While, Source Monitor panel is used to play the original and source clip; Program Monitor panel is used to play edited videos. Using the Source Monitor panel, you can convert a source clip according to the requirement. You can set the In and Out points, insert clip markers, and trim the clip. In this section, you learn to open and clear a clip using a Source Monitor panel. Later, you get familiar with the time controls present in both the panels. And then, we discuss in detail about the Time code and get you acquainted with the safe zone of a video.

Opening a Clip in the Source Monitor Panel

To see a clip in the Source Monitor panel, you need to import a source clip. Perform the following steps to open the required clip in the Source Monitor panel:

1. **Import** and **select** a clip (Wildlife.wmv). Then **double-click** the selected clip. In our case, we have double-clicked Wildlife.wmv clip. As the result, the clip opens in Source Monitor panel.

2. Click the **Play-Stop Toggle** button in the bottom-middle of the Source Monitor panel to view the clip. The clip starts to play in the Source Monitor panel.

Similarly, you can open multiple clips in the Source Monitor panel. Alternatively, to open the source clip, drag it from the Project panel to the Source Monitor panel.

Closing a Clip in the Source Monitor Panel

As required, you can either close a single clip or all the clips opened in the Source Monitor panel. In our case, we are closing a single clip named: 001.jpg. Perform the following steps to close a clip:

1. Click the **Source** menu under the Source Monitor panel, as shown in picture 1.6 with the red arrow. It opens a dropdown list on the screen.

2. **Select** a clip that you want to close. In our case, we select 001.jpg.

3. **Click** the Source menu under the Source Monitor panel again.

4. Select **Close** option. As the result, the selected clip closes.

Picture 1.6

Exploring Time Controls

The panels, Source Monitor and Program Monitor, contain similar time controls to view a clip. The only difference between both the panels is, while the Source Monitor panel is used to view a source clip, the Program Monitor panel is used to view edited clip. The time controls, are shown in picture 1.7.

Picture 1.7

Let's briefly discuss the main time controls present in the monitors:

- **Time ruler:** Helps you to view the total time duration of the clip. You can view the time code in other formats and icons to represent markers and In and Out points.
- **Current Time indicator (CTI):** Refers to the small blue-triangle that displays the position of the current frame of the clip.
- **Current-time display:** Displays the time code for the current frame and are located at the bottom left of each monitor. While the Source Monitor panel displays the current time of the opened clip, the Program Monitor panel displays the current time of the sequence.
- **Viewing area bar:** Refers to thin bars with curved handles located above the time ruler. This bar represents the visible area of the time ruler and allows scaling of time.
- **Duration display:** Shows the total time duration of the sequence.

Apart from these main time controls, there are some other controls present in the time controls box. Those controls are marked with numbers in the picture 1.8, and explained below in detail referring by the number:

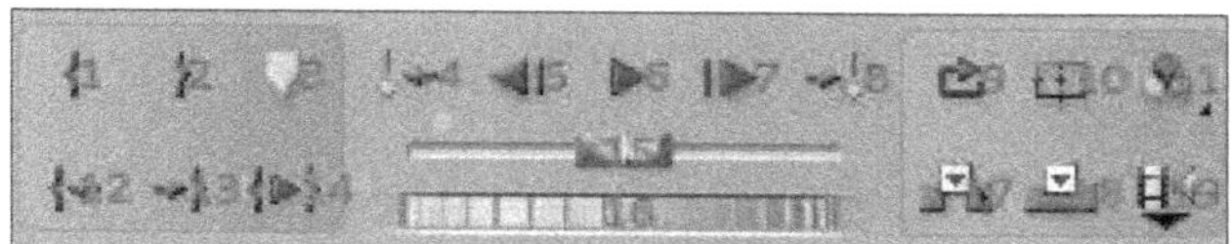

Picture 1.8

Commonly used time controls

Number	Time Controls	Description
1	Set In Point (I)	Marks the In point of a video. In other words, the Set In point marks the starting point of the video.
2	Set Out Point (O)	Marks the Out point of a video. In other words, the Set Out point marks the end point of the video.
3	Set Unnumbered Marker (Num*)	Creates a marker in the video for future reference.
4	Go To Previous Edit Point (Page Up)	Moves CTI to the previous edit in a clip.
5	Step Back (Left)	Allows moving a single frame backward.
6	Play-Stop Toggle (Space)	Allows playing or stopping the clip.
7	Step Forward (Right)	Allows moving a single frame forward.
8	Go To Next Edit Point (Page Down)	Moves CTI to the next edit in a clip.
9	Loop	When selected, plays the video repeatedly.
10	Safe Margins	Allows you to view the margins of the safe zone for a video.
11	Output	Allows you to decide how the output of the clip is produced. By default, the output is selected as Composite Video.
12	Go To In Point (Q)	Moves CTI from the current position to the In point of the video.
13	Go To Out Point (W)	Moves CTI from the current position to the In point of the video.
14	Play In to Out	Plays a video from the In point to Out point.

15	Shuttle	Allows you to play a clip forward and backward with increased playback time.
16	Jog	Allows you to forward and backward a clip by dragging the jog.
17	Lift	Allows you to remove or lift a clip from one location to another and leaves a gap in its place.
18	Extract	Works similar to the Ripple Edit Tool. Using the Extract Tool you can lift a clip from one location to another leaving no gap behind.
19	Export Frame	Opens the Export Frame dialog box that lets you quickly export a video to a location.

Understanding the Time Code

The representation of time duration to keep track of position along the Timeline panel in video editing software is done by the time code. It is displayed as a series of four number groups separated by colons (as in case of Source Monitor panel) and semi-colons (as in case of Program Monitor panel). A sample time code is shown picture 1.9.

Picture 1.9

As shown in the picture above, the time code is divided into four variables. The variables are: hours, minutes, seconds, and frames. These four variables help to keep a detail track of the clip while editing in Premiere Pro.

Viewing Safe Zone

Safe zone is the area defined in the clip, which displays irrespective of the output device the clip is played. For example, consider the case of T.V sets, the signal edges for these are cut. The amount of lost signal varies with different sets. In such a case, it is worth watching the clip in safe zone after the editing is complete in Premiere Pro, as shown in picture 2.0. To view safe zone, click the Safe Margins icon (shown in picture 2.0 with the red arrow. The safe zone is divided into two sections, action-safe zone and title-safe zone.

Picture 2.0

Previewing Media Files

You can preview the clips (media files, such as audio or video) that you import to the project in the Source Monitor panel. In case, you want to import an audio file from the hard drive to the project and preview it in the Source Monitor panel. Perform the following steps to preview medial file:

1. **Import** the audio file that you want to preview. In our case, we import **Sleep Away.mp3** to the Project panel.

2. **Drag** Sleep Away.mp3 to the Source Monitor panel. As the result, the file is moved to Source Monitor panel.

3. Click the **Play-Stop Toggle** button under the Source Monitor to preview the audio. As the result, the audio starts playing.

Trimming a Video Clip in the Source Monitor Panel

Trimming in Premiere Pro is the process of shortening the video as required. To trim the video, set the In and Out point of the video as required. Consider a case, where you want to work or make a video of a particular footage from the complete video. In such a case, Premiere Pro allows you to import the video in the project and trim the desired footage from it. Perform the following steps on your computer to trim a video:

1. **Open** the video that you want to trim in the Source Monitor panel. In our case, we have opened Wildlife.wmv.

2. **Place** the CTI at that point where you want to start the trimmed video from. In our case, we set the time code as: **00:00:20:18**. Then click the **Set In Point (I)** button.

3. **Place** the CTI at the point you want to end the trimmed video. In our case, we set the time code as: **00:00:29:11**. Then click the **Set Out Point (O)** button. As the result, the video is trimmed.

4. **Drag** the trimmed video to the Timeline panel. The video appears in the Timeline panel and in the Program Monitor panel.

5. Click the **Play-Stop Toggle** button to preview the trimmed video. As the result, the trimmed video starts playing.

Looping an Audio or Video Clip

Looping involves playing the clip in a repeated manner. A media file, whether an audio or a video is of a specific duration. By default, when you import and play a clip, it is played only once. However, Premiere Pro allows you to play the desired clip repeatedly in a loop. Perform the following simple steps on your computer to loop a clip:

1. **Open** a clip in the Source Monitor panel. In our case, we open the 001.jpg image sequence in the Source Monitor panel.

2. Click the **Loop** button under the Source Monitor panel of your screen. This way, you activate the Loop button.

3. Click the **Play-Stop Toggle** button to play the clip. As the result, the clip starts to play in a loop in the Source Monitor panel.

Lesson 5
Working with Sequence and Clips

Premiere Pro helps you to edit a movie with ease and comfort. A movie as a whole can be quite long and complex, and hence difficult to edit. In such case, you can divide the movie into sequences and clips. Sequence represents a part of the whole video. Similar to the sub-folders of a project, the clips are components, such as audio, video, still images, or an image group present in the sequences for a complete video.

Several sequences and clips are available for you to work with. You can apply various transitions and effects, trim a clip as required, set different start and end points for them, and extract a specific footage from a complete video. In this chapter, you familiarize with the Timeline panel. Next, you learn to work with tracks and to create a new sequence, nest sequences, and transparent video clip. Further, you learn to add clips and then to work with multiple clips. This chapter also describes the concept of Time Remapping and key frame. Later, you learn to apply a transition and finally, you learn to set parameters using the Effect Controls panel.

Using Timeline Panel

The Timeline panel is one of the commonly used panels in Premiere Pro CS6. Using this panel, you can edit a video. You can drag clips to this panel, animate them, apply various audio and video effects, and transitions, as required. By default, a single Timeline panel appears whenever Premiere Pro is launched or the project is created. The Timeline panel is shown in picture 2.1. A brief description of the components present in the Timeline panel includes:

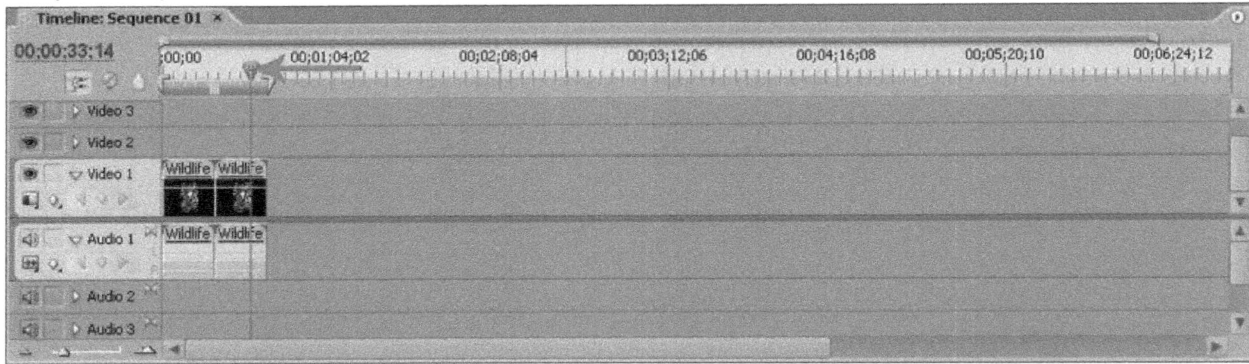

Picture 2.1

- **Sequence tab:** Displays the name of the sequence
- **Time ruler:** Shows the time duration of a clip as the clip progress
- **Video tracks:** Refers to the tracks, where a single video clip or a group of multiple video clips can be placed in a single track or multiple tracks
- **Audio tracks:** Refers to the tracks, where a single audio clip or a group of multiple audio clips can be placed in a single track or multiple tracks

In this section, you learn to work with the Current-Time Indicator that involves the following:
- Moving it manually
- Moving it using the time code
- Moving it to the edge of the clip

Moving the Current-Time Indicator

Premiere Pro allows you to manually move the CTI to any position. You can drag the CTI and play the clip from any location. Perform the following steps to move the CTI manually:

1. **Drag** the CTI to any location, as shown in picture 2.1 with the red arrow. In our case, we move it to 00;00;33;14.

2. **Release** the mouse-pointer. As the result, the CTI is moved to that location in the Timeline panel of your screen.

Moving Current-Time Indicator using the Time Code

Premiere Pro also allows you to move the CIT using the time code. Perform the following steps to move the CTI using the time code:

1. **Click** the time code to set a time for the location where you want to move the CTI. The time code is shown in blue at the top-left corner of picture 2.1.

2. **Type** the time for the location. In our case, we type: **5** seconds. Then **press** the Enter key. As the result, the CTI is moved to the new location along with the video in the Program Monitor panel.

Snapping the Current-Time Indicator to the Clip Edge

You can also move the CTI to the edge of a clip; whether at the start or the end, irrespective of the current position of the CTI. Suppose you are at the middle of a video, which is of longer duration and you just want to view the end rather than the complete video. In such a case, you can move the CTI to the end using the END key from the keyboard. You can also move the CTI to the beginning of a video using the Home key from the keyboard. Perform the following steps on your computer to move the edge of a clip:

1. **Place** the CTI from where you want to move. Then press the **Home** key to move to the beginning of the video.

2. Press the **End** key to move to the end of the video. This way, you have familiarized with the Timeline components and moving the CTI.

Working with Tracks

Premiere Pro provides tracks to work with multiple audios and videos. The concept of different tracks has revolutionized the editing approach. Tracks provide high flexibility while editing clips in Premiere Pro. You can position the clip on a track by moving it to a position and also apply transitions and effects to it. If a portion of a track is changed, it does not affect the underlying or surrounding tracks, as the tracks are isolated in nature. For instance, you can add audio and video effects present on one track without affecting the other tracks.

In this section, you learn to add, delete, and rename tracks. In addition, you get familiar with the track lock feature. Let's begin with adding tracks.

Adding Tracks

Premiere Pro, by default, provides you with three tracks, audio as well as video. However, you can add more tracks if required using the Add Tracks dialog box. Perform the following steps to add tracks in the Timeline panel:

1. Choose **Sequence> Add Tracks** from the Menu bar. It opens the <u>Add Tracks</u> dialog box on the Premiere Pro screen.

2. **Type** the number of video tracks that you want to add in the <u>Video Tracks</u> text box. In our case, we type **2**. Then press the **Enter** key.

3. **Type** the number of audio tracks that you want to add in the <u>Audio Tracks</u> text box. In our case, we type **2**. Then click the **OK** button. As the result, the tracks are added in the Timeline panel.

Deleting Tracks

You can easily delete unwanted tracks from the Timeline panel. Multiple tracks can be confusing sometime. To avoid this, you can remove those tracks that are not required in the project. Perform the following steps to delete a track:

1. Choose **Sequence> Delete Tracks** from the Menu bar. It opens the <u>Delete Tracks</u> dialog box on the screen.

2. Select (put check mark) the **Delete Video Tracks** check box. In case you want to delete an audio track, select the Delete Audio Tracks check box.

3. **Click** the down arrow button under the <u>Video Tracks</u> group to open a dropdown list. Then you need to select **Video 5** (or any) track that you want to delete.

4. Click the **OK** button in the dialog box. As the result, the selected video track Video 5 is deleted from the Timeline panel.

Renaming Tracks

While editing a video in Premiere Pro, you need to rename a track. By default, the present tracks or the newly added ones have a predefined name. However, you can modify the name of these tracks, if required. Renaming tracks allows for easy navigation and searching for the required track. Perform the following steps to rename a track:

1. **Right-click** the track that you want to rename. In our case, we right click Video 1. It opens a context menu on the screen.

2. Select **Rename** option from the context menu of your screen. The default name of the video track is selected.

3. **Type** a name: (Master Video) of the track, and press the **Enter** key. As the result, the selected video track is renamed.

Analyzing the Track Lock Feature

Locking a track is a useful task that prevents you from making unwanted changes to it, while working on a specific sequence. However, the clips present in the locked track can be exported and previewed but cannot be modified. To lock a track, click the **Toggle Track Lock** button beside the name of the track.

Creating a New Sequence

Sequence in Premiere Pro can function as a module of a project or as a sub-folder. However, a sequence can in itself be a complete project. Consider a scenario of a book on a particular field, such as on Multimedia applications. In this book, description of several softwares can be given as different modules, such as Photoshop, Sound Forge, or Flash. Similarly, Premiere Pro is a digital editing application that helps you to create a movie with various video clips of long duration. In such case, it might be possible that changes you made to a single clip affect the other in the same sequence. Therefore, to avoid this, you can edit multiple clips in different sequences and group them in a new sequence after editing all the clips. Perform the following steps on your computer to create a new sequence:

1. Choose **File> New> Sequence** from the Menu bar. It opens the <u>New Sequence</u> dialog box on the screen.

2. **Type** a name of the new sequence in the <u>Sequence Name</u> text box. In our case, we have retained the default name of the sequence that is **Sequence 02**.

3. In the same New Sequence dialog box, click the **Tracks** tab which is at the top-middle. As the result, the Tracks tab is activated.

4. **Type** the number of video tracks that you want in the new sequence in the <u>Video</u> text box. In our case, we type: 1.

5. **Type** the number of audio tracks that you want in the new sequence in the <u>Stereo</u> text box. In our case, we type 1. Then click the **OK** button. As the result, the new sequence **Sequence 02** is created with the specified audio and video tracks.

Nesting Sequences

You can create hierarchies and groups of clips and sequences using the nesting feature available in Premiere Pro. The depth and complexity of nesting sequence depend on the user requirement. A nested sequence functions like a normal sequence; however, the only difference is that the source sequence consists of all the clips, while the nested sequence contains the selected clips. Moreover, the effects, transitions, and trimming can also be done on the nested sequence.

Consider a scenario of a parent and child, where certain qualities in the child are inherited from the parent, but the child can function as an independent entity. Similar to the parent-child relationship, the nested sequence is the derivation of the source sequence; however, its working is similar to any other sequence. Nesting of sequence can be useful for the following: (1) You can reuse the sequence, (2) Apply different settings to the same sequence, (3) Streamline the editing space. Perform the following steps to create a nested sequence:

1. **Import** the required clips in the sequence. In our case, we import **001.jpg** and **Penguins.jpg** to **Sequence 02**.

2. **Select** the clips that you want to copy to a nested sequence. In our case, we select 001.jpg and Penguins.jpg clips.

3. Choose **Clip**> **Nest** from the Menu bar. As the result, the selected clips are nested in the **Nested Sequence 03**.

4. Double-click the **Nested Sequence 03** to open it. When it opens in the Timeline panel, click the **Play-Stop Toggle** button in the <u>Program Monitor</u> panel to view the nested sequence. The nested sequence starts playing.

Lesson 6
Creating a Transparent Video Clip
Using Premiere Pro, you can also create a blank transparent video clip. It is similar to the synthetic video clips, such as Black Video or Bars and Tone. Consider a scene, where you want to show lightning and thunder effect in a movie, the particular footage cannot be shot due to certain reasons. In such case, you can insert a blank transparent clip at an appropriate place in the video and apply the required effects to it. Some of the effects that you can apply to a transparent video clip are Ellipse, Lightning, Paint Bucket, or Grid. Perform the following simple steps on your computer to create a transparent video clip:

1. Select **File**> **New**> **Transparent Video** from the Menu bar. It opens the <u>New Transparent Video</u> dialog box. In our case, we create the transparent video with the default settings.

2. Click the **OK** button in the dialog box. The Transparent Video is created. Then **drag** the Transparent Video from the Project panel to the Timeline panel.

3. **Release** the mouse-pointer after dragging. Then click the **Play-Stop Toggle** button to preview the Transparent Video clip in the Program Monitor panel.

Working with Clips in a Sequence
Using Premiere Pro, you can easily work with the imported clips in a project. You can edit, modify, select, or delete the clips as required. Suppose, numerous clips are placed in a sequence and you want to arrange them or want to apply effect or transition to a particular clip. In such cases, you can move the clips and drag and drop the required effect from the Effects panel to apply to a clip. In this section, you learn to select and move the clips. Next, you learn how to enable and disable clips. You also learn how to split the clips and to remove the gaps between the clips. Let's begin with selecting and moving clips.

Selecting and Moving Clips
While reviewing your project, you might feel that you have placed some of the clips or a particular clip at a wrong place. In such case, you can select and move the required clip from one location to another. Perform the following steps to select and move a clip:

1. Select the **Selection Tool (V)** from the Tools panel. Selection Tool is the first tool at the top-left in the Tools panel.

2. **Select** the clip that you want to move to a new location. In our case, we select 001.jpg clip. Then **drag** the clip to a location where you want to place it. In our case, we move the clip next to Penguins.jpg clip.

Enabling and Disabling Clips

You can enable or disable a particular clip as required. When a clip is in enabled mode, you can edit it, such as shortening the time duration taken for its processing. While in disabled mode, the clips might be visible, but you cannot preview in the Program Monitor panel or during the export of the clip.

Splitting Clips Using the Razor Tool

Splitting the clips involves dividing a clip into multiple clips, using the Razor Tool in Premiere Pro CS6. The clips that are split function as a full-fledged clip in itself with separate In and Out points. Splitting of clips is useful when you might require a particular footage of the entire clip multiple times. You can cut that specific footage and paste it on a required location. Perform the following steps to split the clip:

1. **Click** the sequence tab (in the Timeline) to open the sequence where the clip to be edited is available. In our case, we open **Sequence 01**. The Sequence 01 tab is activated.

2. Select the **Razor Tool** from the Tools panel. Then **click** in a position, where you want to split the clip. As the result, the clip is split in two different clips at the specified location.

3. **Move** the second clip to a distance from the first clip. Then **click** the Play-Stop Toggle button to view the result.

Removing Gaps between Clips

At times, it might occur that while editing clips in a sequence, space is created between the clips. In Premiere Pro, you can easily remove this unwanted space and play the clip continuously using the Ripple Edit Tool. Perform the following steps to remove gap between clips:

1. **Select** the empty space in the Timeline panel that you want to delete. You can select the empty space that was created in the previous section.

2. Choose **Edit> Ripple Delete** from the Menu bar. As the result, the gap is removed. Alternatively, you can press Shift+Delete to remove the gap.

Working with Multiple Clips

A complete video contains multiple sequences, which generally contains multiple clips of different types, such as audio, video, or still images. You might find it difficult and time consuming to apply effects and edit each single clip individually. In such a case, Premiere Pro allows you to work with multiple clips simultaneously. In our case, we want to change the duration of clips. Perform the following steps to change the duration of clips:

1. **Create** or open a new sequence with multiple clips to change the speed. In our case, we create **Sequence 04** sequence.

2. **Select** multiple clips holding the Shift key down. Then choose **Clip> Speed/Duration** from the Menu bar. It opens the Clip Speed/Duration dialog box.

3. Click the **Duration** text box. Then **type** a value (5 seconds) for the duration, and click the **OK** button at the bottom.

4. **Place** the Current-Time Indicator (CTI) at the end of first clip. Then **check** time code (at the top-left in the Timeline panel) for the total duration of the clip. You will see that the total duration of the clip is 5 seconds which we set in the preceding steps.

Exploring Time Remapping

Using the Time Remapping effect of Premiere Pro, you can change the speed of a video. You can slow down, speed up, or freeze specified portion of a video as required. For example, a video of a man walking, using the Time Remapping effect you can show him moving slowly, or stop him all of a sudden; unlike the Speed/Duration dialog box, which allows you to apply only a constant speed throughout the clip.

However, you can apply the Time Remapping effect only to a video and not to an audio. In other words, if you have applied the Time Remapping effect to a video that consists of an audio as well, then the audio part of the clip remains unaffected. Time Remapping effect can be applied in two ways, either with varying time or with speed transitions. Perform the following steps to apply the Time Remapping effect to a video:

1. **Create** or open a scene that consists of a video to which you want to apply the Time Remapping effect. In our case, we have created a new scene, **Sequence 05** that consists of a video clip.

2. Click the **Clip Effect** menu to open a dropdown list, as shown in picture 2.2 with the red arrow. Then select the **Time Remapping** option, and then select the **Speed** option from the sub-menu.

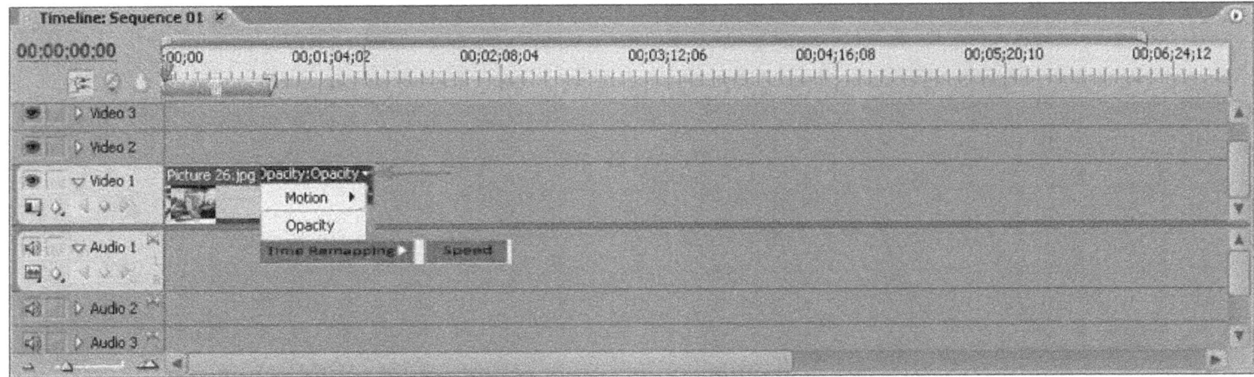

Picture 2.2

3. **Click** to select the position where you want to modify the speed of the clip, while holding the **Ctrl key** down. In our case, we place at the **00;00;13;07** position.

4. **Drag** the rubber band either in the up or down to increase or decrease the speed at the position you have set in the preceding step. In our case, we drag in upper direction to increase the speed to **150.00%**.

5. **Click** the Play-Stop Toggle button to preview the video clip. As the result, the video clip plays faster than the original video clip. Keep in mind that when you increase or decrease the speed of a video clip, the total duration is also changed according to the speed.

Using Markers

Markers are the representation of key places in a clip, such as effect at a particular point in a clip. You can also emphasize the important places in a clip and position or arrange them. Markers can be placed anywhere be it a sequence or a clip. However, these are only for your references and do not affect the video clip. There are three types of markers namely, sequence marker, clip marker, and encore chapter marker. These markers are further categorized as numbered or unnumbered. A single sequence or a clip can include up to 100 (from 0 to 99) numbered markers, while there can be many unnumbered markers, depending on the requirement. The created markers appear as small icons in time rulers of the Program Monitor and Source Monitor panels. While clip markers also appear within the clips in the Timeline panel; sequence markers appear in sequence in the time ruler. In this section, you learn to add an unnumbered marker and move it. Perform the following steps to work with a marker:

1. **Double-click** the clip on which you want to set the marker. In our case, we double-click Wildlife.wmv form Sequence 02. The selected clip opens in the Source Monitor panel.

2. **Place** the Current Time Indicator (CTI) at the position where you want to set the marker in the Source Monitor panel.

3. **Click** the Set Unnumbered Marker (Num *) button. This button is already shown in picture 1.8. As the result, the unnumbered marker is created. Sometimes, it might be possible that the created marker is placed at a wrong position. You can move the marker by dragging it to the required position.

Exploring Video Effects

There are numerous effects in Premiere Pro that you can apply on clips to make them attractive and alluring. Effects include different color adjustments or providing a blur effect. By applying effects to a video clip, you can animate it and make it user-friendly and interactive. These effects are categorized in different folders present in the Effects panel.

The categories include Adjust, Blur & Sharpen, Channel, Color Correction, Distort, Generate, Image Control, Keying, Noise & Grain, Perspective, Stylize, Time, Transform, Transition, Utility, and Video. Each category contains various types of effects. For example, using the Adjust category, you can adjust colors, brightness, and contrast of a clip; using the Color Correction category you can work with colors.

Exploring Key Frames

Key frames are used to define the start and end of different frames to provide a smooth transition of the effect applied between those frames. For example, consider a bouncing ball; the movement of the ball can be defined it terms of key frames. The upward direction of the ball can be defined as one frame and the downward direction of the ball can be defined as another frame. Here are the steps to create key frames for a sequence:

1. **Open** or create a new sequence. In our case, we create a new sequence, **Sequence 06**. Then **import** a video. In our case, we import **Lightning.avi** video.

2. Place the **CTI** where you want to add the key frame. In our case, we place the CTI at the **10th frame**. It is shown in picture 2.3 with the double-red arrow numbered 1.

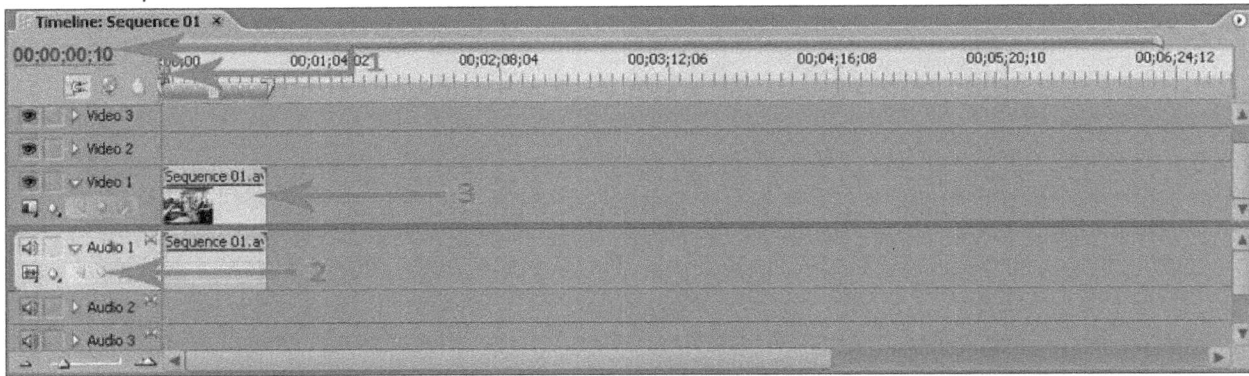

Picture 2.3

3. Click the **Add/Remove Keyframe** button, as shown in picture 2.3 with the red arrow numbered 2. As the result, the required keyframe is added. Similarly, you can create more key frames. In our case, we create three more key frames.

4. **Drag** the yellow line either up or down to set opacity as required (shown in picture 2.3 with the red arrow numbered 3). In our case, we set the opacity of the first frame to 0.

5. Similarly, **set** the opacity of another frame. Then place the **CTI** at the start of the clip, and click the **Play-Stop Toggle** button to play the clip. As the result, the video starts playing, and when the clip nears the end, the opacity of the clip starts decreasing as set according to the keyframes.

Applying Transition on a Clip

Transition defines how you move from one clip to another in a video comprising of multiple clips. By default, when you place clips sequentially, the last frame of one clip is followed by the first frame of another. You can also apply transitions on a video that consists of a single clip; at the start and end of it. Applying transitions between clips make their appearance smooth and presentable. Premiere Pro provides several transitions, such as 3D Motion, Dissolve, Special Effect, or Stretch that you can apply to a video clip. However, you can place a transition effect only at the beginning or end of any clip. Here are the steps to apply a transition:

1. **Open** the video on which you want to apply the transition. In our case, we open **Lightning.avi** present in **Sequence 06**.

2. In the Effect panel (at the bottom-left of the Premiere Pro screen), you need to **click** the arrow beside the Video Transitions bin. It opens a list of child bins.

3. **Click** the arrow beside (3D Motion) any child bin. A list of transition effects present in the **3D Motion** child bin appears.

4. **Select** an effect (Curtain) that you want to apply to the video. Then **drag** the selected effect to the point you want to apply. In our case, we drag the **Curtain** effect to the beginning of the clip. As the result, the Curtain effect is applied at the beginning of the clip. We are also applying another transition effect at the end of the clip.

5. **Select** the effect (Fold Up) that you want to apply at the end of the clip. Then **drag** the selected effect to the end of the clip. The **Fold Up** effect is applied at the end of the clip.

6. **Click** the Play-Stop Toggle button to preview the file. As the result, the video clip starts with a Curtain effect, and then, during the end of clip, the Fold Up effect appears.

Setting Parameters using the Effect Controls panel
Using the Effect Controls panel, you can modify the effects and transitions applied to a clip as required. The required parameters depend on the type of effect that is applied to the clip. Perform the following steps to set the parameter of an effect:

1. Open the **Effect Controls** panel which is at the top-middle beside the Source Monitor panel of the Premiere Pro screen.

2. **Double-click** the effect that you want to modify from the Timeline panel. The parameters related to the selected effect, in our case, the **Curtain** effect appears.

3. In the Effect Controls panel, enable (put check mark) the **Reverse** check box to reverse the action of the effect. Then **click** the Play-Stop Toggle button to preview the clip.

Lesson 7
Working with Audio
Using Premiere Pro, you can work with audio clips with ease in the similar manner you work with the video. You can perform several editing operations on the audio clip, such as trimming the clip to the required duration and unlinking the audio clip from the corresponding video clip to which its is attached. In addition, you can also apply various effects and transitions to a clip using the Effects panel as there are different categories in the form of folders. Tracks that are added to the project can be mono, stereo, or 5.1 surround channels. The mono track consists of one audio channel; the stereo track consists of two audio channels; while the 5.1 track consists of three front audio channels, two rear channels, and a single two-frequency effect (LFE) audio channel that is connected to a subwoofer. In this chapter, you familiarize with the Audio Mixer panel. Moving further in the chapter, you learn about the audio files in a project. Then, you explore the audio effects. In the end, you learn to edit the available audio, such as linking/unlinking, adjustment of volume level, and the DeNoiser effect.

Exploring Audio Mixer
You can perform all the editing operations in Timeline panel or Audio Mixer panel. Using the Timeline panel, you can apply effects and transitions directly to a clip; while the Audio Mixer panel allows you to customize the applied clip effects as required. Using the Audio Mixer panel (shown in picture 2.4), you can modify the settings simultaneously, while listening to an audio and viewing a video. The list below describes the components of the Audio Mixer panel which are numbered in red in the picture:

Picture 2.4

(1) Panel menu: Opens a dropdown menu that consists of general options related to the panel, such as Undock Panel and Close Panel.

(2) Time code: Displays the complete time-duration of a clip.

(3) Track name: Displays the name of a track.

(4) Automation mode: Consists of five options; Off, Read, Write, Latch, and Touch according to which the track is played. A brief description of these options:

> **Off:** Plays the audio without interference of the key frames. Moreover, the changes made to the track are not stored when the Off automation mode is selected
>
> **Read:** Considers the key frames as well during the audio playback
>
> **Write:** Keeps a record of all the modifications made on the track and creates corresponding key frames in the Timeline panel
>
> **Latch:** Records modifications similar to the Write option. However, the automation starts only after a clip property is adjusted
>
> **Touch:** Similar to the Latch option, except that when you stop adjusting a property, its options returned to the earlier state set before the recording

(5) Pan/balance control: Balances the channel playback of a clip.

(6) Mute Track, (7) Solo Track, (8) Enable Track for recording buttons: Enables you to work with individual tracks. The Mute Track button puts off the audio, the Solo Track button mutes rest of the tracks and allows you to listen to a group of tracks, and the Enable Track for recording button allows you to record the audio in the selected track.

Master VU meter and fader: Displays all the tracks and their output signal levels.

(9) Go to In Point: Moves the Current-Time Indicator (CTI) to the set In Point in the clip.

(10) Go to Out Point: Moves the CTI to the set Out Point in the clip.

(11) Play-Stop Toggle: Plays or stops the whole audio clip.

(12) Play In to Out: Plays the audio clip from the In point to the Out point.

(13) Loop: Plays the clip in a repeated manner when selected.

(14) Record: Enables you to record the audio with the use of headphones.

After learning about Audio Mixer panel, let's now learn to use Audio files available in a Premiere Pro project.

Using Audio Files in Premiere Pro

The audio files are one of the indispensable components if you want to make a complete video. The use of audio files appropriately can make the video effective and interactive to a project. Consider a scenario, where you have a video clip containing an audio and you want to customize it as required. In such a case, you can make certain modifications, such as trimming or extraction. You can also mix multiple audios and loop them to play it repeatedly. In this section, you learn to add audio files present in the project to the Timeline panel. Next, you learn to mix audio files and trim the audio file as required. You also learn to extract an audio from a video clip and loop a clip.

Adding Audio Files to the Timeline Panel

Using Premiere Pro, you can easily add audio files to a project to make an impressive video. Perform the following steps to add an audio file to the Timeline panel:

1. **Create** or open the sequence to which you want to add the audio file. In our case, we create a new sequence, **Sequence 07**.

2. **Import** the required audio file that you want to add to the Timeline panel. In our case, we import the **Maid with the Flaxen Hair** audio file.

3. **Drag** it to the Timeline panel in the required track. As the result, the specific audio file is added to the Timeline panel.

Trimming an Audio File

Sometimes the duration and length of an audio file does not fit to the length of the video. It might be possible that the audio is of longer duration than the video. In such a case, you can trim the audio file to shorten the duration to fit to the length of the video. Perform the following steps to trim the audio file:

1. **Double-click** the audio file to open it in the Source Monitor panel. Then place the **CTI** at the position where you want to specify the **Set In Point (I)**. In our case, we place the CTI at the position **00:00:30:00**.

2. In the buttons-set below the Source Monitor panel (shown in picture 1.8), click the **Set In Point (I)** button to set the starting point of the audio. It sets the starting point at the **00:00:30:00** time code.

3. Place the **CTI** at the position where you want to specify the **Set Out Point (O)**. In our case, we place the CTI at the position **00:02:30:00**. As the result, the end point of the trimmed audio is set at the **00:02:30:00** time code and the audio is trimmed.

4. Click the **Play In to Out** button to play the trimmed clip. Now you will see that the audio is trimmed to suit the length of the associated video.

Extracting Audio from a Video Clip

In case you want to use only the audio from a particular video, you can extract only the audio part. This extracted audio file appears in the Project panel as a separate clip that can be used whenever required. By default, the name of the clip remains the same as the video clip from which it is extracted and is appended with **Audio Extracted**. Perform the following steps to extract an audio from a video clip:

1. **Select** a video clip from which you want to extract the audio, in the **Project** panel. In our case, we select Wildlife.wmv.

2. Choose **Clip> Audio Effects> Extract Audio** from the Menu bar. The Extract Audio dialog box appears showing the extraction progress. After the extraction is complete, the extracted audio with the default name appears in the Project panel.

Looping an Audio File

Looping is performing a function repeatedly until it is stopped manually. Similar to a video file, an audio file can also be played repeatedly in a project using Premiere Pro. Perform the following steps to loop an audio file:

1. **Double-click** the audio file that you want to loop in the Timeline panel. Then click the **Loop** button in the buttons-set below the Source Monitor panel.

2. **Click** the Play-Stop Toggle button below the Source Monitor panel to preview the result. You will see that the audio file plays in a loop.

Working with Audio Effects

Similar to the video effects, there are numerous effects and transitions for an audio. All these effects and transitions are categorized into several folders such as 5.1, Stereo, Mono, Crossfade. These folders are present in the Effects panel and further consist of wide range of effects that can be applied to an audio. You can view these effects by expanding the specific folder. Perform the following steps to apply an effect to an audio:

1. **Select** the audio file to which you want to apply an effect. In our case, we select Maid with Flaxen Hair.mp3 audio file.

2. In the Effect panel (at the bottom-left of the Premiere Pro screen), you need to **click** the arrow beside the Audio Effects bin to expand it in the Effects panel. It opens a list of child bins.

3. Click the arrow beside the **Stereo** child bin to expand it. Then **select** the effect (Bass), and **drag** the selected audio effect to the audio in the Timeline panel.

4. **Click** the Play-Stop Toggle button to preview the file. As the result, the audio file with the Bass effect is played.

Editing an Audio in Premiere Pro

In Premiere Pro, editing involves operations such as volume adjustment, linking and unlinking of clips or removal of extra noise from an audio. In professional video editing for movies, you need to edit the audio files. In this section, you learn to: (1) unlink and link the clips, (2) adjust the volume of an audio using the Timeline panel, (3) adjust the volume of an audio using the Effects Control panel, and (4) applying the DeNoiser Effect.

Unlinking/Linking Video and Audio Clips

At times, you might want to use the audio and video parts of a clip, separately in a project. In such case, Premiere Pro allows you to unlink the audio and video of a clip, using the Unlink option. You can unlink a clip in two ways, either by using the Clip menu or by the context menu that appears when you right-click a clip. In our case, we are unlinking the clip using the Clip menu. Similarly, you can also link the unlinked audios and videos of the same clip or of different clips as required. Perform the following steps to unlink a clip:

1. **Select** the clip that you want to unlink. In our case, we select Wildlife.wmv. Then choose **Clip> Unlink** from the Menu bar. As the result, the audio and video files are unlinked.

2. **Move** the video file. You can see on your screen that only the video part of the Wildlife.wmv movie is moved.

At times, you may want to apply the same effect to a group of audio and video files. Applying the same effect to different individual clips can be tedious. In such case, you can link the required clips using the Link option. Perform the following steps to link clips:

1. **Select** the clips that you want to link. In our case, we select the Wildlife.wmv audio and Wildlife.wmv video files.

2. Choose **Clip> Link** from the Menu bar of your Premiere Pro screen. As the result, both of the files are linked.

Adjusting Audio Volume using the Timeline panel

At times, you may want to increase or decrease the volume of an audio. You can easily adjust the volume for a clip as required. Perform the following steps to adjust the audio volume using the Timeline panel:

1. **Click** the Show Keyframes button which opens a dropdown list, as shown in picture 2.5 with the red arrow numbered 1.

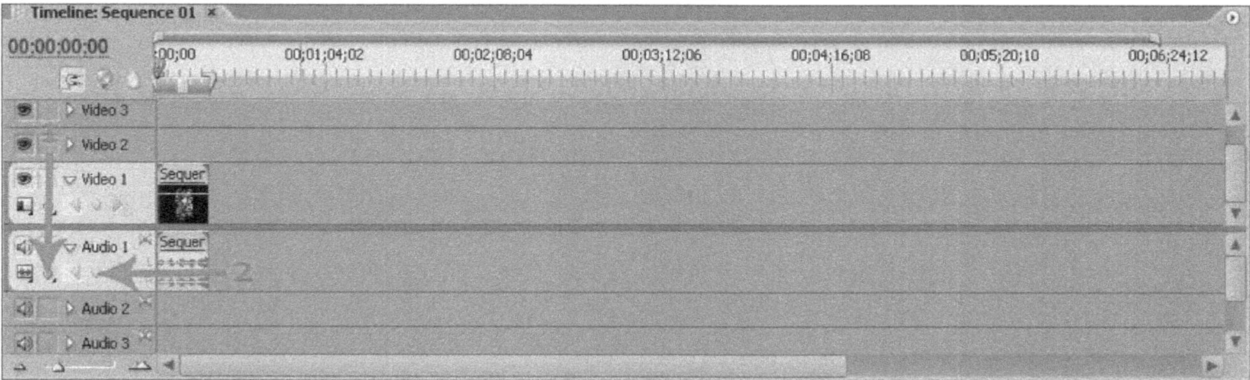

Picture 2.5

2. In the dropdown list, select the **Show Track Volume** option. Then place the **CTI** at the position where you want to add the key frame. In our case, we place the CTI at **00:00:01:16**.

3. Click the **Add-Remove Keyframe** button, as shown in picture 2.5 with the red arrow numbered 2. As the result, the key frame is added. Similarly, you can add more key frames.

4. **Drag** the yellow band of a frame to increase or decrease the volume. Then place the **CTI** at the beginning of the clip, and **click** the Play-Stop Toggle button to preview the audio file.

Adjusting Audio Volume using the Effect Controls panel

In the preceding section, you learnt to adjust the volume in the Timeline panel; however, you can also adjust the volume for an audio using the Effect Controls panel. Perform the following steps to adjust the volume using the Effect Controls panel:

1. **Select** an audio file, and click the **Effect Controls** tab to activate the panel. Then click the arrow beside the **Volume** audio effect to expand it.

2. Click the arrow beside the **Level** option. The properties present under the Level option appear in the panel.

3. **Drag** the volume slider to the required level. As you can see on your screen, the yellow band in the Timeline panel is moved up. You can play the audio to preview the effect.

Applying the DeNoiser Effect

Consider a scenario, where you are recording an audio during which, some distracting noise interferes, such as a phone ringing. However, you need to continue with the recording with that sound. In such a case, after recording, import the audio in Premiere Pro and apply the DeNoiser effect to it. This effect can detect extra noise in an audio and remove it. This effect can be applied to any audio whether 5.1, Stereo, or Mono clip. You can also customize the DeNoiser effect by making changes to its options. A brief description of the options is as follow:

- **Noisefloor:** Displays the decibel level of a clip when it is played.
- **Freeze:** Recognizes the noise that is played and stopped frequently in a clip. Moreover, the calculation of the estimated noise floor can also be stopped.
- **Reduction:** Sets a value for the extra noise to be reduced, between the range: 20 to 0 dB.
- **Offset:** Determines the offset value between the automatically detected value of the noise floor and the user-defined value. This offset value can range between: -10 and +10 dB.

After knowing about the options of the DeNoiser effect, you need to perform the following steps to apply the DeNoiser effect:

1. **Select** the audio clip on which you want to apply the DeNoiser effect. Then select the **DeNoiser** effect from the <u>Effects</u> panel (not the Effect Controls panel) which is at the bottom-left of the Premiere Pro screen.

2. **Drag** the effect to the selected clip. As the result, the DeNoiser effect is applied and its options appear in the Effect Controls panel.

Lesson 8
Working with Titles in Premiere Pro

In designing and editing applications, titles play a significant role while presenting information in the form of characters or symbols in different languages, such as English, Japanese, French, and Chinese. A title guides a reader about what exactly the document or file (video clip file) conveys. Therefore, Premiere Pro CS6, a digital video editing application, has built-in features that support the use of text. It provides the Title Designer Window, which you can use to create a wide variety of text and graphics. Further, you can import and superimpose over existing video or can also run as a single video clip having text and graphics. Digital video is the most informative and intensive modes of communication that uniquely displays video with textual information. The title directly conveys the main objective to interpret the required information. The digital videos with titles help industries such as films, news broadcasts, archive live footage, and technical learning. For example, the production of movies can only be accomplished if their crew member's names are displayed. Title also plays a major part to present the opening and closing credits of a film in the form of running subtitles, and the spoken words of presenters, actors, and this is almost the main part for any production houses.

In this chapter, you learn to create still, rolling, and crawling titles. Further, you learn to edit titles, which involve formatting text, drawing shapes, transforming objects, aligning and distributing objects in titles. You also learn to show or hide video behind the title. Next, you learn to use the path type tool using which you can type text on a specified path. In addition, you learn to work with text effects followed by adding sheen, strokes, and shadow effects. Towards the end, you learn to add various pre-defined text styles to the titles.

Creating Titles using Adobe Title Designer

In Premiere Pro CS6, you can create titles for video clips in three ways; Still title, Roll title, and Crawl title using the Title Designer Window. This window has many text and graphics tools and is divided into **Title Tools**, **Title Actions**, and **Title Styles**, **Title**, and **Title Properties** panel. These panels are used for developing a wide variety of designs in titles, whether static, rolling, or crawling. You can also create broadcast-quality video clips or sequence that includes text and graphic elements using the Title Designer Window. Titles in Premiere Pro CS6 are automatically added to the active bin in the Project panel. The titles are saved as part of the project; those titles created in the Title Designer Window appear in the Project panel of the UI. You can also import titles from external files with .prtl extension. These imported titles are automatically saved with the project.

Creating a New Still Title

In Premiere Pro CS6, you can create titles in a video clip by inserting a text. To create a title, you need to select Title> New Title> Default Still from the Menu bar. These titles can be placed at any location in the video clip with the desired text fonts installed on your system. Perform the following steps to create a still title in a video clip:

1. **Create** a new project in Premiere Pro CS6. Then choose **File**> **Import** from the Menu bar. It opens the Import dialog box on the screen.

2. Navigate **Libraries**> **Videos** under the left pane of the Import dialog box. Then double-click the **Sample Videos** folder under the right pane of the Import dialog box.

3. Select the **Wildlife** video in the Import dialog box, and click the **Open** button at the bottom. The video file is imported and appears in the Project panel.

4. Under the Project panel, **select** the Wildlife.wmv imported video file, and **drag** and **drop** it in the Timeline panel.

5. **Drag** the Viewing area bar in the Timeline panel to modify the current duration of the imported video clip, as shown in picture 2.6 with the red arrow numbered 1. In our case, we drag the Viewing area bar to the end of the video clip.

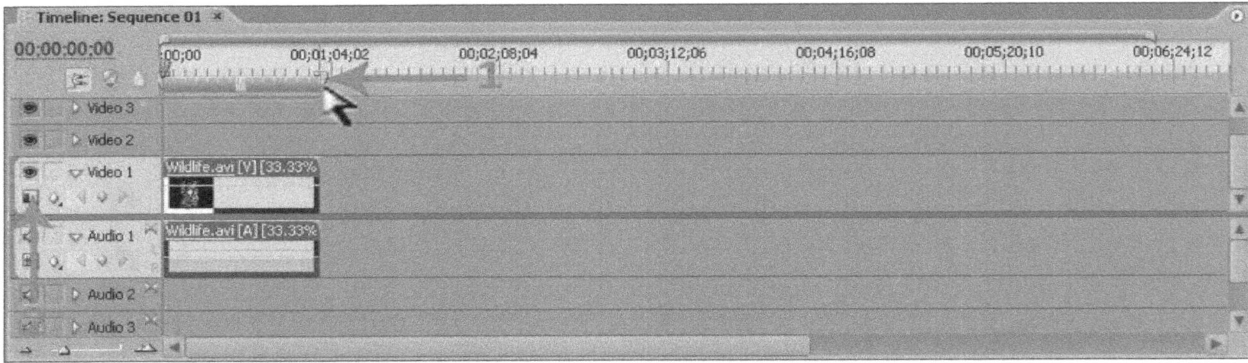

Picture 2.6

6. Click the **Set Display Style** button in the Timeline panel, as shown in picture 2.6 with the red arrow numbered 2. Then select the **Show Frames** option from the dropdown list.

7. Choose **Title> New Title> Default Still** from the Menu bar to open the New Title dialog box. Then **type** a name in the Name text box. In our case, we have retained the default name as: Title 01.

8. Click the **OK** button in the New Title dialog box. It opens **Title Designer Window** on the screen, as shown in picture 2.7.

9. **Click** at a location between the wired spaces enabled under the Title Designer Window. Then **type** a text (**Nature**) at the location, as shown in picture 2.7.

10. Click the **Close** button to close the Title Designer Window. As the result, the **Title 01** appears under the Project panel.

Picture 2.7

11. Select the **Title 01** clip under the <u>Project</u> panel. Then **drag** and **drop** the clip in the Timeline panel of your screen.

12. **Drag** the right end of the clip to extend it to the end of the video clip, so that the title text appears in the entire video clip. If you cannot extend the video clip, then right-click on the video clip in the Timeline panel, select Speed/Duration, click next to Duration, enter duration number, and click the OK button.

13. Press the **Spacebar** key on the keyboard to play the video. You will see that the new title appears in the entire video clip.

Creating a New Roll Title

In Premiere Pro CS6, you can create a roll title, which moves from the center vertical axis of the video clip. To create a roll title, you need to select Title> New Title> Default Roll option from the Menu bar. You can adjust the roll settings from top-to-bottom or from bottom-to-top. However, by default it is from bottom-to-top. Perform the following steps to create a rolling title in a video clip:

1. **Create** a new project in Premiere Pro CS6. Then **import** a video (Wildlife.wmv) in the Timeline panel of your screen.

2. **Drag** the viewing area bar in the Timeline panel to resize the present duration of the imported video clip.

3. Click the **Set Display Style** button in the Timeline panel to open a dropdown list. Then select the **Show Frames** option from the dropdown list.

4. Choose **Title> New Title> Default Roll** from the Menu bar. Then **type** a name in the <u>Name</u> text box, or you can use the default name as Title 01.

5. Click the **OK** button in the New Title dialog box of your screen. It opens the **Title Designer Window** on the screen.

Picture 2.8

6. **Click** at a location between the wired spaces enabled under the Title Designer Window. Then **type** a text at the location.

7. Click the **Roll/Crawl Options** button at the top-left of the Title Designer Window, as shown in picture 2.8 with the red arrow at the top.

8. Enable (put check mark) the **Start Off Screen** check box under the **Timing (Frames)** category. Then enable the **End Off Screen** check box under the **Timing (Frames)** category.

9. Click the **OK** button in the Roll/Crawl Options dialog box. Then click the **Close** button to close the Title Designer Window. The **Title 01** appears under the Project panel.

10. **Select** the Title 01 clip under the Project panel, and **drag** and **drop** it in the Timeline panel. Then **drag** the right end of the Title 01 clip to extend it till the end of the video clip, so that the title text appears in the entire video clip.

11. Press the **Spacebar** key to play the video clip with the rolling text. As the result, the video clip appears with the rolling text.

Creating a New Crawl Title

In Premiere Pro CS6, you can create a crawl title that moves from the center horizontal axis of the video clip. You need to specify a left-to-right or right-to-left direction. However, by default crawling is done from left-to-right. Perform the following simple steps on your computer to create a crawling title in a video clip:

1. **Create** a new project and **import** a video file in the Timeline panel. Then **drag** the viewing area bar under the Timeline panel to modify the current duration of the imported video clip.

2. Click the **Set Display Style** button in the Timeline panel, which opens a dropdown list. Then select **Show Frames** option form the dropdown list.

3. Choose **Title> New Title> Default Crawl** from the Menu bar. Then **type** the desired name in the <u>Name</u> text box, and click the **OK** button. It closes the New Title dialog box and opens the Title Designer Window.

4. **Click** at a location between the wired spaces enabled under the Title Designer Window. Then **type** a text at the location.

5. Click the **Roll/Crawl Options** button at the top-left of the Title Designer Window. It opens the Roll/Crawl Options dialog box on the screen.

6. Enable (put check mark) the **Start Off Screen** check box under the **Timing (Frames)** group. Then enable the **End Off Screen** check box under the **Timing (Frames)** group.

7. Click the **OK** button in the Roll/Crawl Options dialog box. Then click the **Close** button to close the Title Designer Window. The **Title 01** appears under the Project panel.

8. **Select** the Title 01 clip under the Project panel, and **drag** and **drop** it in the Timeline panel. Then **drag** the right end of the Title 01 clip to extend it till the end of the video clip, so that the title text appears in the entire video clip.

9. Press the **Spacebar** key to play the video. As the result, the video clip appears with the crawling text. Now you can save this project to use in the next section. For this, choose File> Save and type the file name as: **Crawling Title**.

Lesson 9
Editing Titles
In Premiere Pro CS6, there are several features that help to change or edit the appearance of titles in a video clip. For example, you can change the format by selecting the required font size, style, and color. Titles can also be represented with simple graphical shapes, such as circles, ovals, and arcs. Editing of title also includes the positioning, alignment, distribution of various text objects created in the Title Designer Window. In this section, you learn to format text, draw shapes, transform objects, align and distribute objects in a title. You also learn to show or hide video behind the title.

Formatting Text in a Title
Formatting the text in a title refers to modifying the appearance and arrangement of the text of a title. There are several adjustable options, such as font styles, underlining, caps, and many more to enhance the text of titles. You can also import a font size and style when preparing a video clip for a specific purpose, such as news reading, broadcasting, and technical learning as there are predefined spaces for displaying defined content. Perform the following steps to format text in a title:

1. **Open** an existing project (**Crawling Title.prproj**), which you had created in previous section. Then double-click the **Title 01** in the Project panel to open it in the Title Designer Window.

2. **Double-click** on the title text to select it. Then, in the <u>Title Properties</u> panel which is on the right side in the window, **click** the down arrow beside the **Font Family** option under the <u>Properties</u> group. It opens a dropdown list on the screen.

3. **Select** a font style for the selected title from the list. In our case, we select **Blackadder ITC** style. Then select the checkbox beside the **Small Caps** option under the Properties group.

4. Select the checkbox beside the **Underline** option under the Properties group. Then click the **Close** button to close the Title Designer Window.

5. Press the **Spacebar** key on the keyboard to play the video clip. As the result, the video plays with the formatted title.

Drawing Shapes in Titles
In Premiere Pro CS6, you can draw simple graphical shapes using the drawing tools available under the Title Tools panel in the Title Designer Window. You can create squares, rounded squares, circles, ovals, lies and polygons. You can also use the drawing tools to create outlined shapes or filled shapes. Perform the following steps to draw graphical shapes:

1. **Open** an existing project, and double-click **Title 01** in the Project panel to enable formatting of the title text. It opens the Title Designer Window on the screen.

2. Select the **Arc Tool** in the <u>Title Tools</u> panel which is on the left of the Title Designer Window. Then **click** and **drag** to a location to create a shape using the Arc Tool.

3. Click the **Close** button to close the Title Designer Window. Then press the **Spacebar** key to play the video. As the result, the new shape along with the title appears in the entire video clip.

Transforming Objects in Title

You can modify the font style, size, color, and rotation of titles. You can also change the settings related to the transformations of titles using the Title Properties panel in the Title Designer Window. In the Title Properties panel, there are several adjustable options, such as x-position, angle, height, width, and color for making the required transformations. Perform the following steps to transform objects in a title:

1. **Open** an existing project, and double-click **Title 01** in the Project panel to enable formation of the title text. It opens the Title Designer Window on the screen.

2. **Type** a value for the horizontal position of the title text in the **X Position** text box under the Title Properties panel. In our case, we type **345.0** value.

3. **Type** a value for the vertical position of the title text in the **Y Position** text box under the Title Properties panel. In our case, we type **135.0** value.

4. **Type** a value for the width of the title text in the **Width** text box under the Title Properties panel. In our case, we type **300.0** value.

5. **Type** a value for the height of the title text in the **Height** text box under the Title Properties panel. In our case, we type **110.0** value.

6. **Type** a value for the angle of rotation for the title text in the **Rotation** text box under the Title Properties panel. In our case, we type **10.0** value.

7. Click the **Close** button to close the Title Designer Window. Then press the **Spacebar** key to play the video clip. As the result, the specified transformation along with the title appears in the entire video clip.

Aligning and Distributing Objects in Titles

Positioning objects as you require helps to organize the objects of a title. Positioning involves aligning them either with each other or in relation to the area provided in the Title Designer Window. Depending on the need, you can position objects to the left, center, or right of the Title Designer Window. In Premiere Pro CS6, the center and edges of the objects are considered while aligning them. On the other hand, distributing objects refers to the positioning of objects in a given space, based on the center point, height, and width of the objects. Perform the following steps to align and distribute objects in a title:

1. **Create** a new project, and choose **Title> New Title> Default Still** from the Menu bar. It opens the New Title dialog box on the screen.

2. **Type** a name in the <u>Name</u> text box, or you can retain the default name as **Title 01**. Then click the **OK** button in the New Title dialog box. It opens the Title Designer Window.

3. In the <u>Title Tools</u> panel which is on the left of the Title Designer Window, select the **Ellipse Tool**. Then **click** and **drag** to a location to create a shape using the Ellipse Tool.

4. Select the **shape** using the <u>Selection Tool</u> which is in the Title Tools panel. Then hold the **Alt** key on the keyboard, and **drag** and **drop** the selected shape to a location for creating copies of the drawn ellipse. Similarly, create three more copies of the ellipse.

5. Hold the **Shift** key down and **select** all the five ellipses. Then select the **Vertical Center** option which is under the <u>Align</u> group in the <u>Title Actions</u> panel (at the lower-left) of the Title Designer Window.

6. Select the **Horizontal Center** option under the <u>Distribute</u> group in the <u>Title Actions</u> panel of the Title Designer Window. It will align all the selected objects in a horizontally centered position. Then click the **Close** button to close the Title Designer Window.

Show or Hide Video behind the Title

In Premiere Pro CS6, you can show or hide a video clip on which a text is superimposed. The Show Background Video button under the Title panel allows you to temporarily show or hide the video in the Title Designer Window. When you hide a video, only the title and objects drawn in the Title Designer Window appear. This helps you to work with numerous titles in a single video clip by displaying or hiding the video as required. Perform the following steps to show or hide a video behind the title:

1. **Open** an existing project, and double-click **Title 01** under the <u>Project</u> panel to enable formatting of the title text. It opens the Title Designer Window on the screen.

2. In the <u>Title</u> panel which is at the top-middle of the Title Designer Window, select the **Show Background Video** button. Then click the Close button to close the Title Designer Window.

Using the Path Type Tool

In Premiere Pro CS6, you can add text along the path of an object. The path can be either open or closed. An open path is where the starting and ending points are not connected and a closed path is where the starting and point and ending point are connected. You can also create your own path by drawing lines or curves and add text for titles across the paths. Perform the following steps to use the path type tool:

1. **Create** a new project, and choose **Title> New Title> Default Still** from the Menu bar. It opens the New Title dialog box on the screen.

2. **Type** a name in the <u>Name</u> text box, or you can retain the default name as **Title 01**. Then click the **OK** button in the New Title dialog box. It opens the Title Designer Window.

3. In the <u>Title Tools</u> panel which is on the left of the Title Designer Window, select the **Path Type Tool**. Then **click** at a location within the available space to specify the first point for the path.

4. **Click** at another location to specify the second point for the path. Then again, click at a different location to specify the third point for the path.

5. In the <u>Title Tools</u> panel which is on the left of the Title Designer Window, select the **Convert Anchor Point Tool**. Then **click** and **drag** the middle point of the created path to give smoothness.

6. In the same <u>Title Tools</u> panel, select the **Type Tool**, and **click** anywhere between the path you have drawn. The Type Tool automatically blinks at the initial point of the path where you are allowed to type a text.

7. **Type** a text across the path you have drawn. Then click the **Close** button to close the Title Designer Window.

Working with Text Effects

Text effect is a collection of character formatting attributes, such as font style, color, and size that can be applied to the selected titles under the Title Designer Window. In Premiere Pro CS6, text gives an emphasis to display the title, information or intimate the significant facts in the video and can be used as a header or footer to cover the entire video clip. You can also adjust various properties, such as size, angle, opacity, and color for the text effects. The text effects are added to enhance the appearance of the titles resulting in an appealing look rather than giving a standard style of text. In this section, you learn about text effects, such as sheen, stroke, and shadow. You also learn to add predefined text styles to titles. Let's first learn to add text effects.

Adding Text Effects

You can apply various special effects, such as sheen, stroke, and shadow to title texts. Sheen effect allows you to create a stripe of colored light across the surface of an object. This effect is used to apply a finishing moment to attract the title, by generating a shining streak onto the object. Stroke effect allows you to create inner and outer strokes with other options, such as height, width, and color for filling the respective strokes. You can also add shadow effect to text objects in the Title Designer Window. To do this, select the object and then click on the shadow option under the Title Properties panel. In this section, you first learn to add sheen effect, then you learn to add strokes effect, and finally, you learn to add shadow effect to the title.

Adding the Sheen Effect

In Premiere Pro CS6, you can add sheen effect to titles in a video clip. This effect creates a stroke line between the title text with several other adjustable properties, such as color, opacity, and size. Perform the following steps to add text effects (Sheen) to the title:

1. **Open** an existing project, and double-click **Title 01** in the <u>Project</u> panel to enable formatting of the title text. It opens the Title Designer Window on the screen.

2. In the <u>Title Properties</u> panel which is on the right side of the Title Designer Window, you need to **click** the arrow (▶) beside the **Sheen** option under the <u>Properties</u> group. It opens several editing options under Sheen option.

3. Click the check box beside the **Sheen** option to enable editing options for Sheen effect in the Title Properties panel.

4. Click the color box beside the **Color** option under the <u>Sheen</u> group to select an alternate color for the Sheen effect in the Title Properties panel.

By default, the color for the Title appears White. It opens the **Color Picker** dialog box which is divided into a color shade selection plane, color range slider, and color value text boxes.

5. **Click** on a color that you want in the color shade selection plane. Then click the **OK** button to close the Color Picker dialog box.

6. **Type** a value (**50**) in the <u>Size</u> text box under the **Sheen** group in the Title Properties panel. Then **type** a value (**10**) in the <u>Angle</u> text box under the **Sheen** group in the Title Properties panel.

Adding the Strokes Effect

In Premiere Pro CS6, you can add strokes to the title text in two ways, by applying inner strokes and outer strokes. These can be further edited with various other options such as type, size, color, and opacity. Perform the following steps to add text effects (Strokes) to the title:

1. **Create** a new project in Premiere Pro CS6. Then **create** a new title and type **Stroke Effect** in the Title Designer Window.

2. Click the **Add** underlined text beside the <u>Inner Strokes</u> option under the <u>Strokes</u> group in the Title Properties panel of the Title Designer Window.

3. Click the color box beside the **Color** option under the <u>Strokes</u> group in the Title Properties panel to select color for the inner stroke. It opens the **Color Picker** dialog box on the screen.

4. **Click** on a color that you want from the color shade selection plane. Then click the **OK** button to close the Color Picker dialog box.

5. Click the **Add** underlined text beside the <u>Outer Strokes</u> option under the <u>Strokes</u> group in the Title Properties panel of the Title Designer Window.

6. Click the color box beside the **Color** option under the <u>Strokes</u> group in the Title Properties panel to select a color for the **outer stroke**. It opens the **Color Picker** dialog box on the screen.

7. **Click** on a color that you want from the color shade selection plane for the outer stroke. Then click the **OK** button to close the Color Picker dialog box. As the result, the text appears with the stroke effect applied on it.

Adding the Shadow Effect

You can add shadows to the title texts. Shadows can be further edited with other options, such as color, opacity, angle, distance, and spread. Here are the steps to add shadow effects to the title:

1. **Create** a new project in Premiere Pro CS6. Then **create** a new title and type **Shadow Effect** in the Title Designer Window.

2. Click the check box beside the **Shadow** option under the <u>Properties</u> group in the <u>Title Properties</u> of the Title Designer Window.

3. Click the color box beside the **Color** option under the <u>Shadow</u> group in the <u>Title Properties</u> panel to select a color for the shadow. It opens the Color Picker dialog box on the screen.

4. **Click** on the color that you want from the color shade selection plane for the shadow. Then click the **OK** button to close the Color Picker dialog box.

5. **Type** a value (**90**) in the <u>Angle</u> text box under the <u>Shadow</u> group in the Title Properties panel. Then **type** a value (**25**) in the <u>Distance</u> text box under the <u>Shadow</u> group in the Title Properties panel.

6. **Type** a value (**15**) in the <u>Size</u> text box under the <u>Shadow</u> group in the Title Properties panel. Then **type** a value (**10**) in the <u>Spread</u> text box under the <u>Shadow</u> group in the Title Properties panel.

Adding Text Styles

There are several predefined title styles in the Title Style panel in the Title Designer Window. Premiere Pro CS6 has a collection of styles with combinations of color and font characteristics, such as font style, size, and color. The Title Style panel exhibits a preview of the text styles in the form of thumbnails that helps you to quickly apply over numerous titles in a clip. You need to click on a style; it is automatically applied to the title. Perform the following steps to add text styles in the title:

1. **Create** a new project in Premiere Pro CS6. Then **create** a new title and type **Text Styles** in the Title Designer Window.

2. **Select** a style under the <u>Title Styles</u> panel in the Title Designer Window. After you click a style, it is automatically applied and appears in the Title Designer Window.

Lesson 10
Working with Effects and Transitions

Video editing involves manipulating and reallocating distinct video shots to create a single video clip. Editing is usually part of the production process; it involves adjusting the color, luminosity, opacity, transitions, sound mixing, and effects. In Premiere Pro CS6, video editing is done using the effects and transitions over the clips. These clips can further be accustomed with cutting segments and planned sequence. Video editing includes editing segments of motion video clips, special effects, and sound recordings. In Premiere Pro CS6, transition is used to move a scene from one clip to another. There are several transitions that you can apply to a sequence from the Effects panel. Transitions are simply a predefined schematic effect, such as spinning wheel and crossfade. You can also adjust the placement of the transition being applied on the cuts, such as at the beginning, at the center or at the end of the cut. By default, placing one clip side-by-side in a Timeline panel results in a cut, where, the last frame of one clip is followed by the first frame of the next clip. You can apply transitions to the clips using the Effects panel and edit them using the Timeline and the Effect Controls panel. Transitions are available in the Video Transitions and the Audio Transitions bin in the Effects panel. There are several transitions such as, dissolves, wipes, slides, and zooms. These transitions are organized in the bins based on the categorization of their functioning.

This chapter describes about effects and transitions in Premiere Pro CS6. You learn to apply effects to a clip, copy and paste them to a clip, disable or enable effects to a clip, and remove. Next, you learn to apply and edit transitions. You also learn to adjust color in a video clip using the change to color, color balance (RGB), and auto color effects. Further, you learn how composition in Premiere Pro CS6 can be done by adjusting clip opacity and using blend modes. Towards the end, you learn about keying effects, such as the Alpha Adjust, Chroma Key, and Matte Key effects.

Understanding Effects and Transitions

Effects and transitions are the integral part of professional video editing. In any video editing application, effect plays a significant role to enhance a video. Effects are setup of predefined values that are used to enhance the brightness, color, contrast, and luminosity of clips. In Premiere Pro CS6, effects are categorized in the Effects panel under Video Effects bin. The effects are applied on the entire video clip. Transitions are by default, setups that are applied between the cuts in a video clip in the Timeline panel; they appear just for a specified time interval over the cut of the videos. In Premiere Pro CS6, you can directly drag transitions from the Effects panel and apply to the Timeline panel over the cut. The default duration of all the transitions is 30 frames and is centered at the cut between two clips. You can change the duration and alignment from the adjustment features available in the Effect Controls panel. You can use an effect to alter the relevance of colors in a video clip, its alignment, distortion between the image clips, and apply artistic effects. In addition, you can also use effects to edit, such as rotate and crop a clip or adjust its size and position within the specified frame in a video clip. Let's briefly learn about the various types of effects available in the Premiere Pro CS6:

- **Fixed effects:** Includes predefined effects that are automatically added to every video clip on the Timeline panel. You can modify these fixed effects from the Effects Controls panel. Fixed effects includes the following effects:
  - **Motion:** Allows you to animate, rotate, and scale clips. You can also adjust the flickering property and can composite them with other clips.
  - **Opacity:** Allows you to adjust the opacity level for the clips. You can also use this effect in overlaying, fading, and dissolving multiple clips.
  - Time Remapping: Allows you to slow down, speed up, or reverse playback, or freeze a frame, for any part of a clip.
  - Volume: Allows you to control the volume for any clip that contains an audio.
- **Standard effects:** Includes additional effects that you can apply on a clip. You can apply these effects from the Effects panel that contains a collection of standard effects. These can be further modified from the Effect Controls panel to adjust the tone and trim pixels of clips. Certain standard effects, such as Four-Point Garbage Matte effect use a direct manipulation from the Source Monitor panel.
- **Clip-based and track-based effects:** Includes all video effects, such as fixed and standard. These effects are used to change separate clips, that impact on individual tracks in the Timeline panel. Track-based effects are applied on the audio of the clips and can be further modified using the Audio Mixer panel to ensure the required output.
- **Effect plug-ins:** Includes effects in the form of plug-ins. You can purchase and apply desired plug-ins from the source. Adobe officially supports only plug-ins that is installed within the Premiere Pro CS6 application.
- **GPU-accelerated effects:** Includes effects that require graphics card for more visual clarity. There are various GPU-accelerated effects, such as Alpha Adjust, Basic 3D, Color Balance (RGB), Color Replace, Crop, Edge Feather, Extract, Gamma Correction, Garbage Matte (4, 8, and 16), Gaussian Blur, Horizontal Flip, Levels, Noise, RGB Curves, RGB Color Corrector, Sharpen, Tint, Track Matte Key, Cross Dissolve, Dip to Black, and Dip to White.
- **High-bit-depth effects:** Includes the video effects and transitions that support high bit depth processing. These effects result in better color cast with high resolution. You can also select the Maximum Bit Depth video rendering option from the New Sequence dialog box to enable this effect.

Working with Effects

In Premiere Pro, effects are applied to video clips in the Timeline panel. You can adjust its various properties by associating it with numbers. You can access these video effects from the Effects panel under the Video Effects bin. This bin provides you a library of pre-defined set of effects, which you can apply on any video clip. Video effects are categorized into a nested structure under the Effects panel with specified named effects. You need to select an effect from the Effects panel and drop it onto the video clip in the Timeline panel. Once you drop the effect on a video clip, you can further edit the associated properties of the selected effect from the Effect Controls panel. In this section, you learn to apply effects to a clip and use the effect presets. You also learn to copy and paste effects to a clip. Next, you learn to disable or enable effects to a clip; and finally, you learn to remove effects from a clip. Let's now learn to apply effects to a clip:

Applying Effects to a Clip

Effects are applied to create potential qualities that are not available in a raw video. There are effects such as, a softening focus, giving a sunset tint to the scene, and making color balancing in a video clip track. You can apply any of these effects to a video clip. In addition, you can apply the same effect multiple times to a single clip with different settings. In Premiere Pro, by default, when you apply an effect to a clip, it remains active for the entire duration of the clip. You can use keyframes to start and stop the effect at specified intervals of time or make the effect penetrating over specified time duration. Perform the following steps to apply effects to a clip:

1. **Create** a new project and **import** a video file in the Timeline panel. Then **select** a frame from the video clip by placing the **CTI** over the clip in the Timeline panel.

2. **Right-click** the selected frame of the video clip. It opens a context menu on the screen. Then select the **Scale to Frame Size** option from the context menu.

3. Select the **Effect Controls** panel at the top. Then **type** values for positioning the selected clip from the video in the Position text box under the Motion video effect in the Effect Controls panel. In our case, we type **594.0** and **305.0**.

4. **Type** a value for scaling the selected clip from the video in the Scale text box under the Motion video effect in the Effect Controls panel. In our case, we type **165.0**.

Using Effect Presets

You can apply effect from the Effects panel that contains a collection of effect presets. You can save time by applying a preset effect on a video clip, rather than manipulating and adjusting each value under the effect settings. For example, you can apply Fast Blur effect on a video clip to quickly blur the entire video. Perform the following steps to use effect presets:

1. **Create** a new project and **import** a video file in the Timeline panel. Then **select** a frame from the video clip by placing the **CTI** over the clip in the Timeline panel.

2. **Right-click** the selected frame of the video clip. It opens a context menu on the screen. Then select the **Scale to Frame Size** option from the context menu.

3. In the <u>Effects</u> panel which is at the bottom-left of the Premiere Pro screen, click the arrow beside the **Presets** bin.

4. Click the arrow beside the **Bevel Edges** child bin under the <u>Presets</u> bin in the Effects panel. Then select the **Bevel Edges Thick** effect under the <u>Bevel Edges</u> child bin of the Presets bin.

5. **Drag** and **drop** the selected effect from the <u>Effects</u> panel to the <u>Timeline</u> panel over the video clip. Then select **Effect Controls** panel which is at the top of the Premiere Pro workspace. Here, the Bevel Edges preset effect appears with more options.

6. Type a value in the **Edge Thickness** text box under the <u>Bevel Edges</u> video effect. In our case, we type **0.20**. As the result, the <u>Source Monitor</u> panel appears with beveled thickness across the edges in the entire video clip.

Copying and Pasting Effects to a Clip

The effect applied on a video clip can further be applied to another video clip. To do this, you need to copy the effect from the source clip and paste it on another video clip. Perform the following steps to copy and paste effects from one video clip to another:

1. **Open** a new project and **import** a video file (Wildlife.wmv) in the Timeline panel. Then **select** a frame from the video clip by placing the **CTI** over the clip in the Timeline panel.

2. **Import** one more video clip (Lightning.avi). Then **drag** and **drop** this (second) video clip also in the Timeline panel. As you can understand, for copying and pasting effects from one video clip to another, you need at least two video clips on the <u>same</u> timeline.

3. **Right-click** the first video clip to open a context menu. Then select **Copy** option from the context menu. It copies the attribute (not the entire video) of the fist video clip.

4. **Select** the second video clip, and **right-click** on it to open the context menu. Then select **Paste Attributes** option from the context menu.

As the result, the effect (attribute) applied on the first video clip (Wildlife.wmv) is copied to the second video clip (Lightning.avi). The **Effect Controls** panel shows the Bevel Edges option that ensures the effect is copied along with the attribute values from one clip to another.

Disabling/Enabling Effects to a Clip

Premiere Pro CS6, you can disable or enable any effect applied on a video clip. The **Toggle the effect on or off** button in the Effect Controls panel allows you to temporarily disable or enable the effect. You can also track the disabling and enabling feature by adjusting the keyframes on a specific duration between the video clips. Perform the following simple steps on your computer to enable and disable effect from a video clip:

1. **Open** an existing video clip on which an effect is already applied. Then click the **Effect Controls** panel at the top of the Premiere Pro CS6 screen.

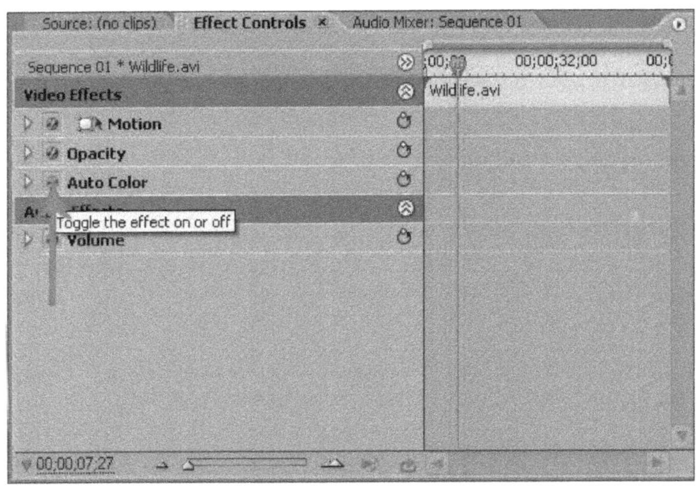

The Effect Controls panel shows the name of the effect which is already applied on the video clip you have opened. And beside the name of the effect, there is **Toggle the effect on or off** button (shown in picture (2.9).

2. Click the **Toggle the effect on or off** button in the Effect Controls panel to disable the effect applied to the video clip.

As the result, the Program Monitor panel on your screen will show the video clip with disabled effect.

Picture 2.9

Removing Effects from a Clip

The effects applied on a video clip can be removed permanently. While working with multiple video clips, certain effects applied to them appear inappropriate; you can remove those effects from the clip. By removing an effect, the video clip again comes in its raw form. If required, you can further apply any effect on that clip. Perform the following steps to remove effects from a video clip:

1. **Open** an existing video clip on which an effect is already applied. Then **select** a frame from the clip by placing the **CTI** in the Timeline panel.

2. **Right-click** the selected frame of the video clip. It opens a context menu on the screen. Then select the **Remove Effects** option from the context menu. The Remove Effects dialog box appears on the screen with all the available check boxes selected by default.

3. Click the check box beside the **Motion** option to clear it. Then click the check box beside the **Opacity** option to clear it. And then, click the **OK** button to close the Remove Effects dialog box. As the result, the effect is removed from the video clip.

Lesson 11
Working with Transitions

Transitions are refined stylized movements that give a special effect in digital video clips. Transitions can be applied on the breaking points known as cuts between the frames of the video clips. As you know that Premiere Pro CS6 is a video editing application, the transitions are schematic effects that you can apply between the breaking points of the video clips. Normally, scenes shot individually, is arranged in a sequence to form a video clip. You can apply transitions between the shots by phasing out one and phasing in another. Premiere Pro facilitates you with several transitions that you can apply to sequences captured or shot, such as wipes, zooms, and dissolves. You can access these transitions from the **Effects** panel and edit using the Timeline and Effect Controls panel. In this section, you learn to apply transitions to a video clip, use Radial Wipe and Venetian Blinds. In addition, you learn to edit transitions applied on a video clip. Let's learn to apply transitions on video clips.

Applying Transitions

You can apply transitions only between two clips, which are effected at the end of one clip and the beginning of another. In addition, you can apply a transition at the middle of a cut, and the two video clips must be on the same track with no spacing between them in the Timeline panel. Transitions are useful, if you want to focus on the general flow of a video clip. While playing multiple transitions over several video clips, transitions might appear to be overlapped. This results in mixing and patchy video effects. To overcome these defects, transitions must be applied on a specified location and between the categorized frames of video clips. Those frames used at the end of the first clip are called tail materials. Those frames affected by transitions at the beginning of the next clip are called head materials. In this section, you learn to Radial Wipe and Venetian Blinds transitions to a selected video clip. Let's now learn to use the radial wipe.

Using the Radial Wipe

The Radial Wipe transition effect can be applied on a location over the cut in the Timeline panel. This effect is enabled under the Wipe child bin of Video Transitions bin in the Effects panel. Perform the following steps to apply the radial wipe transition on a video clip:

1. **Create** a new project and **import** two videos in the Project panel on which you want to apply the transition.

2. **Drag** and **drop** both the videos in the Timeline panel one next to another. Then **select** a frame from the video clip by placing the **CTI** in the Timeline panel.

3. Click the arrow beside the **Video Transitions** bin in the <u>Effects</u> panel to open up various video transition effects.

4. **Drag** the vertical scroll bar (which is on the right of the panel) to the required transition effect under the Effects panel. Then click the arrow beside the **Wipe** child bin under the <u>Video Transitions</u> bin in the Effects panel.

5. Select the **Radial Wipe** transition effect under the <u>Wipe</u> child bin. Then **drag** and **drop** the selected Radial Wipe effect from the Effects panel to the <u>Timeline</u> panel. The Transition message box appears indicating insufficient media and directs that the recently used transition will contain repeated frames.

6. Click the **OK** button to close the Transition message box. As the result, the video transition is applied between the two videos. The CTI is placed over the transition (that is applied between the two video clips). The transition appears at the end of the first video and before the second video starts.

Using the Venetian Blinds

You can apply Venetian Blinds effect on a cut over a video clip in the Timeline panel. You can access Venetian Blinds effect under the Wipe child bin of the Video Transitions bin in the Effects panel. Perform the following steps to apply the venetian blinds transition on a video clip:

1. **Create** a new project and **import** a video file in the Timeline panel. Then select the **Razor Tool** from the <u>Tools panel</u> at the top of the Premiere Pro screen.

2. **Select** a location on the video clip where you want to apply a cut using the Razor Tool, as transitions can be applied only over a cut. You can go ahead and **mark** a cut on the video.

3. Select the **Selection Tool** from the Tools panel. Then **click** the arrow beside the **Video Transitions** bin in the <u>Effects</u> panel.

4. Click the arrow beside the **Wipe** child bin. Then select the **Venetian Blinds** wipe effect from the <u>Wipe</u> child bin.

5. **Drop** the selected Venetian Blinds effect over the marked cut on the video clip in the Timeline panel. Then **double-click** this video transition in the Timeline panel. This activates the <u>Effect Controls</u> panel at the top with various editable options of the selected transition.

6. Type a value in the **Border Width** text box. In our case, we type **7.0**. As the result, the Venetian Blinds video transition appears from the initial point.

Editing Transitions

After applying transitions to the video clips, you may want to edit certain properties, such as timings, alignment, and copy the same transition effect, so that the video clip appears exactly the way you want it. In Premiere Pro CS6, to edit a video clip, select the transition effect from one location and paste it on another location within the video clip. Therefore, you can change the location and alignment of transitions, thereby, changing the look of a video. In this section, you learn to copy, paste, and align transitions. Let's learn to copy and paste a transition.

Copying and Pasting a Transition

You can copy any transition effect in a sequence and paste it in a different location over the cut within the same track in the Timeline panel. Perform the following steps to copy and paste a transition:

1. **Create** a new project and **import** two videos in the Project panel on which you want to apply the copy-paste transition command.

2. **Drag** and **drop** both the videos in the Timeline panel one next to another. Then select the **Razor Tool** from the Tools panel.

3. **Select** a location on the video clip where you want to apply a cut using the Razor Tool, as transitions can be applied only over a cut. You can go ahead and **mark** a cut on the video.

4. **Select** a transition from the <u>Effects</u> panel. In our case, we select the **Center Peel** video transition effect under the <u>Page Peel</u> child bin.

5. **Select** a frame from the video clip by placing the **CTI** in the Timeline panel. In our case, we select the end of the first video clip.

6. **Drag** and **drop** the <u>Center Peel</u> video transition effect from the Effects panel to the Timeline panel over the marked frame by the CTI.

7. Choose **Edit> Copy** from the Menu bar. Then **select** another frame from the video clip by placing the **CTI** in the Timeline panel. In our case, we select the second video clip where the cut was marked using he Razor Tool.

8. Choose **Edit> Paste** from the Menu bar. As the result, the same transition is pasted over the selected location.

Aligning the Transition

You can align the transition effects applied on a cut in three ways: Center at Cut, Start at Cut, and End at Cut. Perform the following steps to align a transition using the Start at Cut option:

1. **Create** a new project and **import** a video file in the Timeline panel. Then **select** a frame from the video clip by placing the **CTI** in the Timeline panel.

2. **Mark** a cut at a location over the video clip in the Timeline panel using the Razor Tool. In our case, we mark a cut at the start of the fifth frame.

3. Select the **Selection Tool** from the Tools panel. Then **select** a transition from the Effects panel. In our case, we select the **Curtain** video transition effect under the 3D Motion child bin.

4. **Drop** the selected video transition from the Effects panel to Timeline panel over the marked frame by the CTI.

5. Double-click on the **Curtain** transition applied over the video clip. It activates the Effect Controls panel at the top with several adjustable options of the selected transition.

6. Click the down arrow list beside the **Alignment** option in the Effect Controls panel. Then select the **Start at Cut** option from the dropdown list.

7. **Type** a value in the Duration text box to increase or decrease the duration of the transition applied over the video clip. In our case, we type **00:00:06:00**.

8. Select the check box beside the **Show Actual Sources** option in the Effect Controls panel. As the result, the modified video appears with all the modifications.

Adjusting Color in a Video

In Premiere Pro CS6, you can adjust the color of an entire video clip. The various color balance effects helps you to alter the levels of hue, lightness, and saturation in the frames of the video clip. Hue specifies the color scheme of the image. Lightness specifies the brightness of the image. Saturation specifies the intensity of colors in an image. Use the Color Correction effect to correct and adjust the color as required. On using this effect, you can solve problems related to the smearing of colors, color range, mixed lighting, highlighting, and shadows. You can preview the modifications in the Source Monitor panel that helps you to easily convey each modification you implement. In this section, you learn to use the change to color, color balance, and auto color effect. Let's first learn to use the change to color effect.

Using the Change to Color Effect
The Change to Color effect helps you to change a selected color from the source clip to a color of your choice. You can adjust this effect further with the options available, such as tolerance sliders for hue, lightness, and saturation to exactly match the color you want. Perform the following steps to use the change to color effect:

1. **Create** a new project and **import** a video file in the Timeline panel. Then **select** a frame from the video clip by placing the **CTI** in the Timeline panel.

2. In Effects panel, you need to **select** a video effect. In our case, we select the **Change to Color** option under the Color Correction effect of Video Effects.

3. **Drop** the selected **Change to Color** video effect from the Effects panel to the Timeline panel. Then select the **Effect Controls** panel at the top of the Premiere Pro screen.

4. **Select** the arrow beside the Change to Color video effect in the Effect Controls panel. Then **click** the eyedropper icon beside the **From** option to select a color from the video clip that you want to change.

5. Then, in the Program Monitor panel, **select** a color from the video clip by clicking with the eyedropper. You can click on anything in the video in the Program Monitor panel just to pick a color. In our case, we select brown color from an animal's face in the video.

6. Then, in the Effect Controls panel, **click** the color box beside the **To** option that opens a **Color Picker** dialog box. There you can replace any color with the selected color.

The Color Picker dialog box appears on the screen. This dialog box is divided in a color shade selection plane, color range slider, and color value text boxes.

7. **Drag** the color-range slider to a preferred color. Then **select** the desired color (dark blue) that you want in the color shade selection plane.

8. Click the OK button to close the Color Picker dialog box. As the result, the animal's face is replaced by the selected color.

Using the Color Balance (RGB) Effect
In Premiere Pro CS6, the Color Balance (RGB) effect helps you to change the amount of red, green, and blue color cast of the frames in a video clip. Perform the following steps to use the color balance effect:

1. **Create** a new project and **import** a video file in the Timeline panel. Then **select** a frame from the video clip by placing the **CTI** in the Timeline panel.

2. In Effects panel, select the **Color Balance (RGB)** option which is under the Image Control effect of Video Effects.

3. **Drop** the selected Color Balance (RGB) video effect form the Effects panel to the Timeline panel. Then select the **Effect Controls** panel which is at the top of the Premiere Pro screen.

4. **Click** the arrow beside the <u>Color Balance (RGB)</u> video effect in the <u>Effect Controls</u> panel to display its various adjustable properties.

The Color Balance (RGB) video effect has three adjustable properties namely: Red, Green, and Blue that allows you to select the color range for a video clip. By default, all the three adjustable properties have a value of 100.

5. **Type** the value (160) in the <u>Red</u> text box under the Color Balance (RGB) video effect in the Effect Controls panel. Then **type** the value (150) in the <u>Green</u> text box. And then, **type** the value (200) in the <u>Blue</u> text box.

As the result, the color of the selected video clip is balanced according to the new values you entered for Red, Green, and Blue color range.

Using the Tint Effect

You can apply the Tint effect to alter the color evidence of an image. By applying this effect, all the colors present in the video clip blends with two colors, namely black and white. Tint effect saturates the entire video clip by decolorizing it into black and white display. The steps to use the auto color effect:

1. **Create** a new project and **import** a video file in the Timeline panel. Then **select** a frame from the video clip by placing the **CTI** in the Timeline panel.

2. In <u>Effects</u> panel, you need to select the **Tint** option which is under the <u>Color Correction</u> effect of <u>Video Effects</u>.

3. **Drop** the selected <u>Tint</u> video effect form the Effects panel to the Timeline panel. Then select the **Effect Controls** panel which is at the top of the Premiere Pro screen. As the result, the Tint effect is applied on all the frames, giving it a black and white color.

Lesson 12

Composition in Premiere Pro CS6

Composition is a technique that enables you to collect some of the source videos to make a final mix. It helps you to select various scenes from individual videos and collaborate it in a single video clip. In Premiere Pro, to composite several video clips, you can apply opacity in clips and adjust various blend modes. For example, in the television commercial advertisement the anchor announces the weather predictions behind the geographical map. This association is done by composition technique. First, the speech of the anchor is recorded in a room with specific background colors, such as blue and green, which a video editing application (Premiere Pro CS6) can remove easily. The background is replaced with the required geographical map as required by the user, and the final video clip is composited with required changes that resemble a common television advertisement. Various movies and computer games with live anchoring use composition technique. Let's first learn to adjust clip opacity.

Adjusting the Clip Opacity

You can easily make a video or graphic track partially transparent by adjusting its opacity value. Thus, the visibility of video clips arranged in different tracks can be adjusted by specifying the opacity value as required. Perform the following steps to adjust the clip opacity:

1. **Create** a new project and **import** two video files one next to the other in the Timeline panel, as shown in picture 3.0.

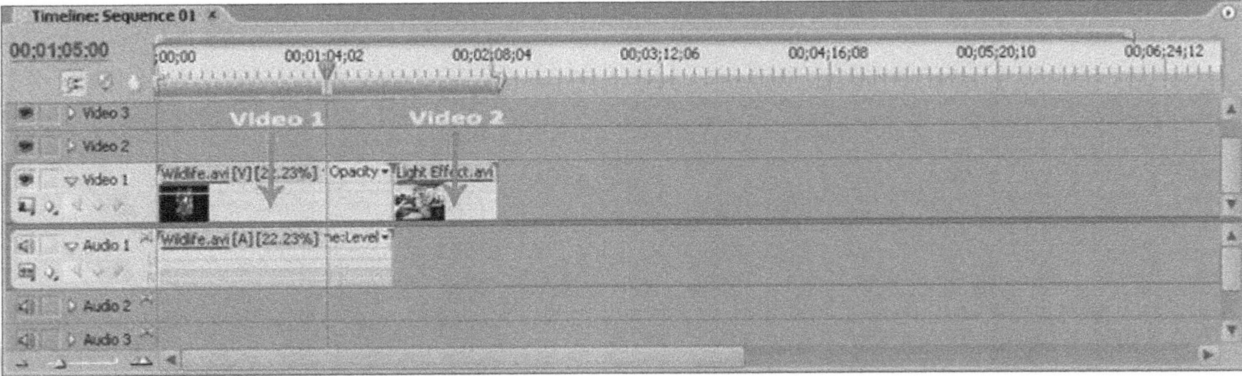

Picture 3.0

2. **Select** a frame from the video clip by placing the **CTI** in the Timeline panel. Then select the **second video** clip from the Video 1 track in the Timeline panel.

3. **Drag** and **drop** the selected video clip from the Video 1 track to Video 2 track in the Timeline panel, as shown in picture 3.1.

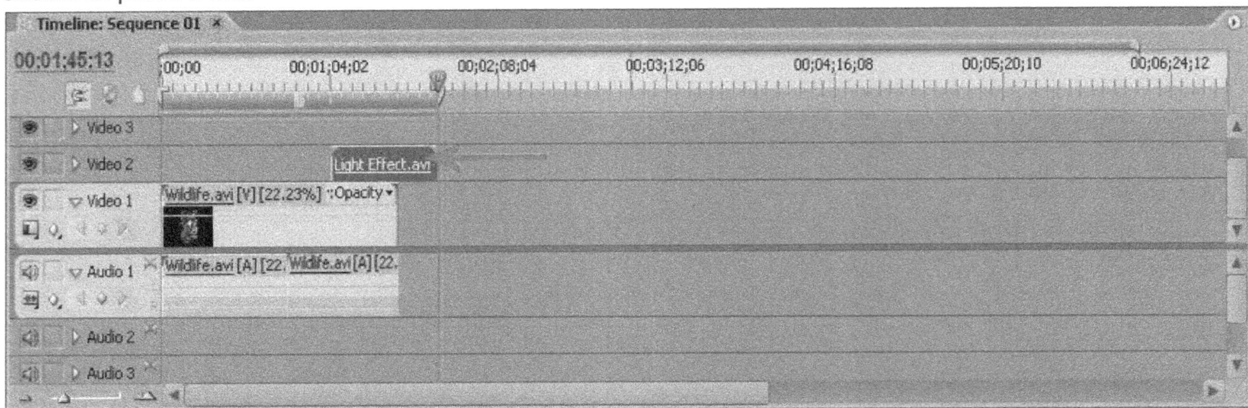

Picture 3.1

4. **Drag** and **adjust** the second video clip in the Video 2 track to the left (half left of first video) in **Video 1** track, as shown in picture 3.1.

5. Select the **Effect Controls** panel from the top of the Premiere Pro screen. Then **click** the arrow beside the **Opacity** video effect in the Effect Controls panel.

6. **Select** the CTI at the start of the second video in the Video 2 track of the Timeline panel. Then **type** the value (**35.0**) in the Opacity text box under the Opacity video effect in the Effect Controls panel of your screen

7. **Select** the CTI at the end of the second video clip in the Video 2 track of the Timeline panel. Then **type** the value (**100.0**) in the Opacity text box under the Opacity video effect in the Effect Controls panel. As the result, the opacity of the **second video** clip is adjusted according to the new values.

Using the Blend Mode

You can superimpose a clip on a track using various blend modes available in Premiere Pro CS6. Blend Modes provide various default setups used to enhance the look of video clips. These blending modes actually merge the tracks by overlapping certain predefined setups, such as Dissolve, Multiply, Color Burn, Hard Light, Soft Light, Saturation, and Luminosity. You can place a video clip on the track higher than a track where another clip is located in the Timeline panel. Select the required blending mode from the options and the Premiere Pro CS6 application automatically superimposes, or blends, the clip in the higher track with the clip placed in the lower track. Perform the following steps on your computer to use the blend mode:

1. **Create** a new project and **import** two video files one next to the other in the Timeline panel. Then **select** a frame from the video clip by placing the **CTI** in the Timeline panel.

2. Select the **second video** clip from the Video 1 track in the Timeline panel. Then **drag** and **drop** the selected video clip from the Video 1 track to Video 2 track in the Timeline panel.

3. **Drag** and **adjust** the second video clip in the Video 2 track to the left (half left of first video) in **Video 1** track, as already shown in picture 3.1.

4. Select the **Effect Controls** panel from the top of the Premiere Pro screen. Then **click** the arrow beside the **Opacity** video effect in the Effect Controls panel.

5. **Click** the down arrow beside the **Blend Mode** option. Then select the **Darken Color** option from the dropdown list. As the result, the video clip with Darken Color blend mode appears.

Working with Keying Effects

Keying is a technical term that finds a defined matching color or brightness pixels from the video clip and make them transparent or semi-transparent. This Keying technique is also used to remove the colored background from a particular scene. You can only remove green and blue background from the scene precisely. For this, you have to usually set up a green/blue screen, and further use the keying tool to make the color transparent. In this section, you learn about the Alpha Adjust, Chroma Key, and Matte Key effects. Let's learn to use the Alpha Adjust effect.

Using the Alpha Adjust Effect

In Premiere Pro CS6, the Alpha Adjust effect is used instead of the Opacity effect. You first need to place two or more video clips in different tracks in the Timeline panel and apply the Alpha Adjust effect to make it partially transparent. The following points describe the Alpha Adjust effect settings for a better understanding of the alpha channel in a clip:

- **Ignore Alpha:** Helps you to ignore the alpha channel of the clip.
- **Invert Alpha:** Helps you to reverse the transparency and opaque areas of the clip.
- **Mask Only:** Helps you to apply the effect only to masked area.

After knowing about the Alpha Adjust effect settings, you can perform the following steps to use the alpha adjust effect:

1. **Create** a new project and **import** a (one) video file in the <u>Project</u> panel. Then import an **image** file in the Project panel.

2. **Drag** and **drop** the <u>video file</u> in **Video 1** track from the Project panel to the Timeline panel. Then **drag** and **drop** the <u>image file</u> in **Video 2** track from the Project panel to the Timeline panel.

3. **Select** a video effect from the <u>Effect</u> panel. In our case, we select the **Alpha Adjust** option under the <u>Keying</u> effect of <u>Video Effects</u>.

4. **Drop** the selected <u>Alpha Adjust</u> video effect from the Effect panel above the <u>image file</u> in Video 2 track in the Timeline panel.

5. Select the **Effect Controls** panel from the top of the screen. Then click the arrow beside the **Alpha Adjust** video effect in the Effect Controls panel.

6. **Select** the check box beside the **Ignore Alpha** option under the <u>Opacity</u> property of the Alpha Adjust video effect in the Effect Controls panel. As the result, the Alpha adjusted video appears with the Ignore Alpha option.

7. Select the check box beside the **Invert Alpha** option under the <u>Opacity</u> property of the <u>Alpha Adjust</u> video effect in the Effect Controls panel. Then, the Alpha adjusted video with **Invert Alpha** option appears on the screen.

8. Select the check box beside the **Mask Only** option under the <u>Opacity</u> property in the <u>Alpha Adjust</u> video effect in the Effect Controls panel. As the result, the Alpha adjusted video with mask only option appears on the screen. At the same time, you can see the effect in the Program Monitor panel also.

Using the Chroma Key Effect
The Chroma Key effect separates all the image pixels that are similar to a specific color. You can select the color value that you want to separate using the Chroma Key effect. After you select a color value from the video clip, it becomes transparent for the entire video clip that you can preview in the Source Monitor panel. You can also make the outlines of the clips smooth by applying feathering through the edges. Perform the following steps to use the Chroma Key effect:

1. **Create** a new project in Premiere Pro CS6 and **import** a video file in the Timeline panel of your Premiere Pro screen.

2. Select a video effect from the <u>Effect</u> panel. In our case, we select the **Chroma Key** option under the <u>Keying</u> effect of <u>Video Effects</u>.

3. **Drop** the selected <u>Chroma Key</u> video effect from the Effect panel to the Timeline panel. Then select the **Effect Controls** panel from the top of the Premiere Pro screen.

4. **Click** the arrow beside the <u>Chroma Key</u> video effect in the Effect Controls panel. Then click the **eyedropper** icon beside the <u>Color</u> option under the Chroma Key video effect. The shape of the mouse pointer changes to an eyedropper icon.

5. **Select** a color from the video clip in the <u>Source Monitor</u> panel. You can click anywhere in the image of the Source Monitor to pick a color.

6. **Type** the value (**7.0**) in the <u>Similarity</u> text box under the Chroma Key video effect in the Effect Controls panel. Then **type** the value (**10.0**) in the <u>Blend</u> text box under the Chroma Key video effect in the Effect Controls panel.

7. **Type** the value (**10.0**) in the <u>Threshold</u> text box under the Chroma Key video effect in the Effect Controls panel. Then **type** the value (**30.0**) in the <u>Cutoff</u> text box under the Chroma Key video effect in the Effect Controls panel. The video clip after applying the Chroma Key effect appears on the screen.

Using the Four Point Garbage Matte Effect

In Premiere Pro CS6, the Four Point Garbage Matte effect helps you to edit the boundary of a selected video clip with four handles across the corners. You can adjust these points by moving it to any location to resize the video clip in the Source Monitor panel. Thus, you can play any video clip by adjusting or resizing it over another video clip. Perform the following steps to use the matte key effect:

1. **Create** a new project and **import** <u>two video</u> files in the <u>Project</u> panel. In our case, we import **Wildlife.wmv** and **LightEffect.avi** video files.

2. Drop the **Wildlife.wmv** video clip on <u>Video 1</u> track of the <u>Timeline</u> panel. Then drop the **LightEffect.avi** video clip on <u>Video 2</u> track of the Timeline panel.

3. **Select** a video effect from the <u>Effect</u> panel. In our case, we select the **Four-Point Garbage Matte** video effect under the <u>Keying</u> child bin of the <u>Video Effects</u> bin.

4. **Drop** the selected **Four-Point Garbage Matte** video effect on the <u>LightEffect.avi</u> video clip on <u>Video 2</u> track of the Timeline panel.

5. Select the <u>Effect Controls</u> panel from the top of the screen. Then **click** the arrow beside the **Four-Point Garbage Matte** video effect.

6. Click the **Four-Point Garbage Matte** video effect in the <u>Effect Controls</u> panel. Now you will see on your screen that the **LightEffect.avi** video clip is accessible with four adjustable corners that help you to adjust the shape and position of the entire video in the <u>Source Monitor</u> panel, as shown in picture 3.2.

7. **Select** and **drag** the four corners in the <u>Source Monitor</u> panel as you desire. In our case, we adjust the corners of the video clip in the Source Monitor panel.

Picture 3.2

8. In the <u>Tools</u> panel which is at the top of the screen, select the **Selection Tool**. Then **place** the cursor at the center of the right vertical side to adjust the size of the video clip, as shown in picture 3.3.

9. **Select** and **drag** the video clip on the specified location to replace it. In our case, we place the video clip towards the upper right corner of the Source Monitor panel.

Now play the video clip to see the video effect. As the result, you will see the Four Point Garbage Matte effect in your video. In the next lesson, you will learn about animation and keyframes.

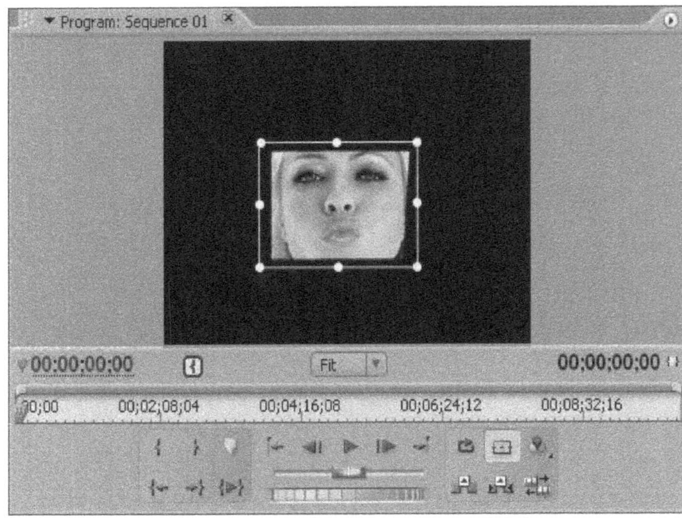

Picture 3.3

Lesson 13
Working with Animation and Keyframes

In Premiere Pro CS6, Timeline panel refers to the area where, you work with various video clips, audio clips, sequences, tracks, keyframes, and blank frames. You can use the Timeline panel to create an animation and edit it with properties, such as opacity, color, brightness and many more. An animation in Premiere Pro CS6 refers to a video clip that is created with collaboration of distinct short video clips or pictured clips, resulting in a single digital video. Using the Timeline panel, you can collect various sound or video clips in the tracks. For example, a cartoon movie is made with a collection of still images and sound clips that are run together very fast to give an illusion of a motion picture. Similarly, animations or videos created in Premiere Pro CS6 contain various tracks and keyframes which, when run together, makes a video clip.

In Premiere Pro, the video and audio clips can be organized and controlled within specified time period using tracks and frames in the Timeline panel. Each frame in a layer presents at a particular time in the animation. Frames contain clips that are placed in the Timeline in a sequence in which the clips would appear in the animation or video. You do not have to place a new clip every time in each frame to create an animation. All clips that are aligned with each other play, resulting in a single video clip. You have to just specify the start and end frames for the video clip or animation.

A keyframe, on the other hand, is a frame or an instance from the video clip that appears in the Timeline panel. It defines the precedence of various clips aligned in a sequence in distinct tracks. Keyframes are required to show any property or effect specific to that location within the video clip or animation. Tracks are similar to multiple filmstrips, stacked one on top of the other, each containing a different image or video and set of images that appear on the Source Monitor panel. A track consists of frames similar to a photographer film with photographic frames. Tracks appear in a row horizontally in the Timeline panel. Frames and keyframes in a track appear over the video clips. In this chapter, you learn about keyframes, wherein, you add, select, move, copy, paste, and delete a keyframe. You also learn to move the Current-Time Indicator to a keyframe. Next, you learn to modify the values of keyframes. Finally, you learn to create an ease in/ease out effect using keyframes. Let's first learn to work with keyframes.

Working with Keyframes

In Premiere Pro, by default, a new project of the first sequence appears with three tracks namely Video 1, Video 2, and Video 3. Video clips injected in Premiere Pro are arranged under the video tracks in the Timeline panel. Initially, when you insert clips in the Timeline panel, by default, they come under Video 1 track. These video tracks are displayed on the left of the Timeline panel, wherein, the video clips are inserted in horizontal rows.

Keyframe animation is one of the simplest and easiest animation techniques. In Premiere Pro, it is suitable for simplest and basic movement of effects and transitions in a video clip. You can manage these transformational changes of clips by setting keys or keyframes. A keyframe refers to a unique state or condition of the object captured at a particular time. In other words, every keyframe signifies a change in one or more attributes of the video or audio clips. As stated earlier, animation can be a sequence of keyframes, in which each frame differs from the previous frame slightly. It is a derivative of time, that is, the changes in an object occur over a period of time. In other words, whenever you change one or more attributes of a clip in a track and record that change using a key, the object is said to be animated. One of the simplest ways to animate an object is through keyframe animation. Using keyframe animation, you can rearrange, delete, and duplicate a key or sequence of keys in the Timeline panel. In this section, you first learn to add a keyframe and then to select and move it. You also learn to copy and paste a keyframe. Next, you learn to delete a keyframe. We also discuss how to move the CTI to a keyframe. Finally, you learn to modify the value for a keyframe. Let's now learn to add a keyframe.

Adding a Keyframe

In Premiere Pro CS6, you can add a keyframe at any location within the video clip in the Timeline panel or in the Effect Controls panel. You can locate the keyframes by placing the CTI at a location in the Timeline panel. In a keyframe animation, the changes in a clip or track attributes are recorded or captured by using the keys or keyframes. Each keyframe corresponds to a particular state of a clip at a particular moment. You need to set the keyframes to animate an object by using keyframes. When you set a keyframe on a clip, the attribute values of the clip are recorded for a particular moment or frame. This implies that when you select the frame, the clip always appears in the same state in which it was when you had set the keyframe. You can set as many keyframes as you want to appropriately animate the clip. Keyframes represent the particular location, where you want to edit certain properties, such as opacity, luminosity, and velocity. Perform the following steps to add keyframes in a video clip:

1. **Create** a new project and **import** a video file in the <u>Timeline</u> panel. In our case, we import Wildlife.wmv video file.

2. **Select** a location for the **CTI** from the video clip where you want to add the first keyframe. Then click the **Add-Remove Keyframe** button (already shown in picture 2.5) from the Timeline panel to insert a keyframe at the location selected by the CTI.

As you click the Add-Remove Keyframe button from the Timeline panel, a round shaped keyframe is automatically added at the location above the yellow line appearing over the entire video clip in the Timeline panel.

3. **Select** a location for the **CTI** from the video clip where you want to add the second keyframe. Then click the **Add-Remove Keyframe** button from the Timeline panel. Similarly, you can add as many keyframes you want.

Selecting and Moving a Keyframe

You can select and move keyframes in the Timeline panel. Keyframes appear as a round shape aligning over the video clip in the Timeline panel. The selected round-shaped keyframes appear filled, whereas, unselected round-shaped keyframes appear hollow. Selecting a keyframe is a simple task; you need to click on a keyframe to select it. Perform the following steps to select and move a keyframe:

1. **Create** a new project and **import** a video file in the <u>Timeline</u> panel. In our case, we import Wildlife.wmv video file.

2. **Add** keyframes at any location in the imported video clip under the Timeline panel. Then **click** on any keyframe appearing in the Timeline panel to select it.

3. **Drag** the selected keyframe towards the left side and **drop** it in a location to reallocate the location. As the result, the selected keyframe is moved to the new location.

Copying and Pasting Keyframes

You can copy the required keyframes and paste them at any location within the video clip in the Timeline panel. For this, you need to copy single or multiple keyframes from the Timeline panel and paste them onto the new location in the Timeline panel. You can also paste the keyframes onto another clip of separate track. When you copy and paste a keyframe, then the values of its attributes are also copied and pasted. The keyframes remain selected after pasting, so you can immediately move them to the target clip. Perform the following steps to copy and paste keyframes:

1. **Create** a new project and **import** a video file in the <u>Timeline</u> panel. In our case, we import Wildlife.wmv video file.

2. **Add** keyframes at a location in the imported video clip under the Timeline panel. Then **click** the first keyframe to select it from the Timeline panel.

3. Hold the **Shift** key from the keyboard to select multiple keyframes. Then select the **second** and **third** keyframes.

4. Choose **Edit> Copy** from the Menu bar to copy the selected keyframes. Then move the **CTI** to a new location where you want to paste the copied keyframes in the video clip.

5. Choose **Edit> Paste** from the Menu bar to paste the copied keyframes. As the result, the copied keyframes are pasted at the new location.

Deleting a Keyframe

You may want to delete an unnecessary keyframe from the Timeline panel. For this, you can use the Clear option in the Edit menu. You can also delete keyframes from the Effect Controls panel. Perform the following steps to delete a keyframe:

1. **Create** a new project and **import** a video file in the <u>Timeline</u> panel. In our case, we import Wildlife.wmv video file.

2. **Add** keyframes at any location in the imported video clip under the Timeline panel. Then **select** the keyframe that you want to delete from the video clip.

3. Choose **Edit> Clear** from the Menu bar to delete or remove the selected keyframe. As the result, the selected keyframe is removed.

Moving the CTI to a Keyframe

You can move the CTI to the keyframes in the Timeline panel. The Effect Controls panel and the Timeline panel, both have the keyframe navigators that help you to precisely place the CTI over the keyframes. You can move them in two directions, namely left and right, that moves to the next and previous keyframes. Perform the following steps to move the CTI to a keyframe:

1. **Create** a new project and **import** a video file in the <u>Timeline</u> panel. In our case, we import Wildlife.wmv video file.

2. **Add** keyframes at any location in the imported video clip under the Timeline panel. Then click the **Go to Next Keyframe** button in the Timeline, as shown in picture 3.4. It will move the CTI over the next keyframe.

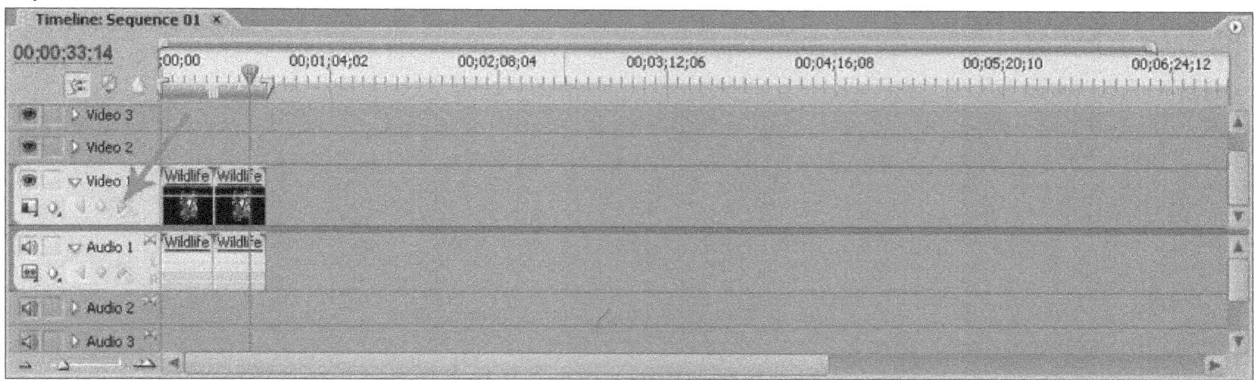

Picture 3.4

3. Click the **Go to Next Keyframe** button again in the Timeline panel to move the CTI to the second keyframe.

4. Click the **Go to Previous Keyframe** button in the Timeline panel to move the CTI over the <u>previous</u> keyframe.

Modifying the Keyframe Values

You can modify the adjustable values, such as opacity, luminosity, and color from keyframes in a video clip. The property and its values can be adjusted from the Effect Controls panel, where you can mark values on the selected keyframes. Perform the following steps on your computer to modify the keyframe values:

1. **Create** a new project and **import** a video file in the <u>Timeline</u> panel. In our case, we import Wildlife.wmv video file.

2. **Add** keyframes at any location in the imported video clip under the Timeline panel. Then select the **Effect Controls** panel from the top of the screen.

3. **Click** the arrow beside the **Opacity** video effect in the Effect Controls panel. Then **click** the arrow beside the Opacity option under the Opacity video effect in the Effect Controls panel.

4. **Select** the second keyframe from the left to modify its position. Then **drag** and **drop** it towards the downward direction.

5. **Select** the fourth keyframe from the left to modify its position. Then **drag** and **drop** it towards the downward direction.

Creating an Ease-In/Ease-Out Effect using Keyframes

Ease-in and Ease-out effect refers to managing the speed in animation technology. While editing your video in Premiere Pro, you need to apply this effect. In all the animation software, such as Adobe Flash and Autodesk Maya, the Ease-in and Ease-out effect is used to enhance the animation quality. In Premiere Pro CS6, you can change the speed of a video clip by creating an ease-in or ease-out effect on keyframes. Ease-in on the keyframe, provides adjustable handles that allow you to create a smooth curve across the keyframe in the Timeline panel. You can also adjust similar curves for ease-out by moving the handles. Thus, you can apply linear or smooth curves to ease-in/ease-out the changes in the playing speed of a video clip. The speed of a clip is referred to as the playback rate of the clip. In the Timeline panel, the clips with speed changes are indicated with a percentage of the original speed. Ease-in slows the value changes entering a keyframe; ease-out gradually fastens the value changes leaving a keyframe. Perform the following steps on your computer to create a fade-in/fade-out effect using the keyframes:

1. **Create** a new project and **import** a video file in the Timeline panel. In our case, we import Wildlife.wmv video file.

2. **Add** keyframes (five keyframes) at any location in the imported video clip under the Timeline panel. Then **select** the second keyframe from the Timeline panel.

3. **Right-click** the selected keyframe to open a list of options. Then select the **Ease In** option from the list that appeared.

4. **Select** the fourth keyframe from the Timeline panel. Then **right-click** the selected keyframe, and select the **Ease-out** option from the list.

5. **Select** both the second and fourth keyframe from the Timeline panel. Then **drag** the right handles of the selected keyframes towards the downward direction.

Now you can see on your screen that the right handles of both the second and fourth keyframes are automatically repositioned.

6. **Drag** the left handles of the selected keyframes towards the left in the downward direction. The left handles of both the second and fourth keyframes are automatically repositioned.

Lesson 14
Rendering and Exporting

In video editing application such as Premiere Pro CS6, rendering is a technique that facilitates a preview of a video after applying various effects, transitions, and adjustments; for example, a motion-picture or a digital video. While rendering a sequence, you need to perform numerous calculations and computations on values of various aspects of the video clips, contained in that project, such as position of the clips, the effects, and the color used in the sequence. Based on these calculations and computations, a single video clip is generated. After assembling and editing distinct video clips in a sequence you can generate the final video. The options you choose while producing the final video depends on the user's requirement.

After preparing a sequence, you need to export a sequence to create a final digital video. The process of translating all the information in a video clip to a final video sequence is called rendering. After you render the sequences of a video clip, export it in any file format. In Premiere Pro CS6, you can render a single video or a sequence of videos. Premiere Pro covers all the video editing elements of a sequence, such as transitions, colors, brightness, luminosity, and effects, which export into a pixel-based digital video file. You can also export the organized video clip in various file formats supported for distinct purposes.

Rendering is a time-consuming process that uses various computer resources, such as RAM, processor, and graphic card, to convert a sequence into a final video. The time consumed to render a scene depends upon other factors, such as type of video used, the number of videos arranged and the color cast of the video. In Premiere Pro, rendering are built-in engines that are specifically used to render a sequence. The highest quality video clips typically take more time to render. The key to work efficiently is to produce good quality videos in a short duration. To save the time, you can render a selected work area or portion of a video clip (that is part of a sequence), that ensures the quality you want for the final output when achieved and then render the entire video clip. In this chapter, we discuss about rendering and previewing in Premiere Pro, which requires defining a work area for rendering and deleting previewed files. Then, you explore various exporting options supported by Premiere Pro. You also learn to use the export settings dialog box, wherein, you explore formats to export and get an overview for export options. Further, the chapter talks about the Project manager, export sequence, nested sequences, and still images. Towards the end, you learn to export video clips for the Web and mobile devices.

Understanding Rendering and Previewing

In Premiere Pro, to export a video requires the rendering process. Rendering refers to collectively gathering all the effects, transitions, and adjustments applied on a video. This process involves lot of calculations and computations to get the desired format of the video. You can apply a sequence or specify a work area for a sequence in the Source Monitor panel. Previewing involves, yielding frames of a sequence for playback. If the hardware is appropriate, previews can be displayed on a compatible National Television System Committee (NTSC) or Phase Alternating Line (PAL) monitor. The delivery of sequences can vary; a sequence with cuts between single tracks of video and audio is delivered quickly, whereas, for sequences that comprise of layered video, audio, and complex effects, rendering requires more processing time. Premiere Pro Real-Time Preview supports all Adobe Premiere effects, transitions, transparencies, motion settings, and titles. If Premiere Pro is unable to obtain the full frame rate of a sequence, you can play the segment at a reduced quality and frame rate.

In Premiere Pro, you can play out the composition of various sections with uniquely defined frame rates. For this, the Timeline panel enables you to define the preview section from the clips, which you want to see before the whole clip renders. The color of the sections indicates their rendering properties, for example, the sections appearing red in color are not rendered, the sections appearing in yellow color does not need to be rendered in the playback, and the sections appearing green in color are rendered. Irrespective of all these indications, you always need to render all the clips in the Timeline panel before you export to render the clip. In this section, you learn to define a work area for rendering and learn to delete previewed files. Let's first learn to define a work area for rendering.

Defining Work Area for Rendering

You can render a defined work area in a video clip. To render a part of an entire video clip, you must define a work area. The sequences with simple effects will be rendered in equitably short time as compared to the video with more effects and transitions. You can adjust the settings to render at a reduced frame rate to reduce time for complicated sequences. The rendered frames appear in a green colored strip in the Timeline panel. In Premiere Pro, the rendering preview generates files on the hard disk. Premiere Pro also creates a preview file that saves time when you export the final video program using the processed effects already rendered. Here are the steps to define a work area for rendering:

1. **Create** a new project and **import** a video file in the <u>Timeline</u> panel. In our case, we import Wildlife.wmv video file.

2. Select the **Work Area Bar** from the <u>Timeline</u> panel to move the bar for defining the work area. The Work Area Bar is shown in picture 3.5 with the red arrow numbered 1. When you select the Work Area Bar, the shape of the mouse-pointer automatically changes into a <u>hand icon</u>.

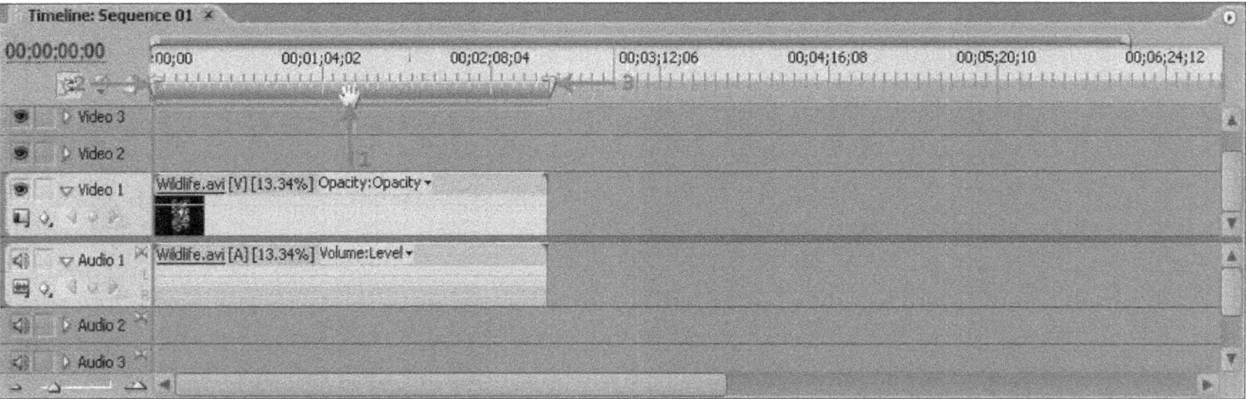

Picture 3.5

3. **Drag** and **drop** the <u>Work Area Bar</u> at any location where you want to define the work area for rendering in the Timeline panel. In our case, we drag and drop it to the right side (one inch to the right side).

4. **Place** the left marker of the <u>Work Area Bar</u> at a location where you want to define the work area for rendering. The left marker of the Work Area Bar is shown in picture 3.5 with the red arrow numbered 2.

5. **Place** the right marker of the <u>Work Area Bar</u> at a location where you want to end the work area for rendering. The right marker is shown in picture 3.5 with the red arrow numbered 2.

6. Select **Sequence> Render Effects in Work Area** from the Menu bar. As the result, the Rendering dialog box appears displaying the progress.

After the defined work area gets rendered, it is displayed with <u>green</u> color bar within the specified work area in the Timeline panel. By the way, you can place the mouse-pointer over the Work Area Bar to display a tool tip that shows the Work Area Bar start timecode, end timecode, and duration of the video clip.

Deleting Rendered Files

In Premiere Pro, you can delete the rendered files. To do this, select Delete Render Files from the Sequence menu of the Menu bar. The rendered frames of the video clip are deleted and you cannot undo this in the same project. Perform the following steps to delete the previewed (rendered) files:

1. **Open** an existing project in Premiere Pro CS6. In our case, we open the same project that we created in the previous section of the lesson.

2. Select **Sequence> Delete Render Files** from the Menu bar. It opens the <u>Confirm Delete</u> message box with a confirmation to delete all the rendered files associated with the current project. This deletion cannot be undone.

3. Click the **OK** button in the Confirm Delete message box. As the result, the rendered files from the video clip are deleted in the Timeline panel; a red colored continuous strip appears in the Timeline.

Exploring Export Options

You can export the prepared video clip using the exporting options. Select a media export format from the seven points, namely **Media**, **Title**, **Tape**, **EDL**, **OMF**, **AAF**, and **Final Cut Pro XML**. To access these options, you need to select **File> Export** and an option from the Menu bar. The various exporting types are defined as follows:

- **Media:** Allows you to export using Adobe Media Encoder and permits you to select an output format in the Export Settings dialog box. The selected format determines the Preset in which you want to export the video clip file. For this, you need to select the format best suited for your needs.
- **Title:** Allows you to export titles from the Premiere Pro CS6 application with the .prtl extension. The title files exported directly into a .prtl extension can be further used in any other sequence by importing them. The imported and exported titles become part of the current project file.
- **Tape:** Allows you to export a sequence or clip to a videotape in a supported camcorder or VTR. You can export to archive a master tape or to deliver rough edits for screening from VTRs using this option.
- **EDL:** Refers to **Edit Decision List** (EDL) that allows you to export a data file, which describes the project and enables you to recreate it, either with related media or using another editing system. In Premiere Pro, you can export a project as an EDL in the CMX3600 format. You can also merge clips that support the standardized EDL format. In this way, the EDL file format enables you to interpret the merged clip sequence track items similar to separate audio and audio clips that are used together in the sequence at the same time location.

- **OMF:** Refers to Open Media Format (OMF) exporting that allows you to export all the active audio tracks from the entire sequence from the Premiere Pro application to OMF file.
- **AAF:** Refers to Advanced Authoring Format (AAF) that allows you to export sequence clips into a multimedia file format. This AAF exporting option helps you to exchange digital media and metadata between platforms, systems, and applications. The data can be written and read by the user applications that supports this AAF format, such as Avid Media Composer.
- **Final Cut Pro XML:** Allows you to export an XML file from Premiere Pro into merged clips. This exporting option allows you to prepare a file into nested sequences in Final Cut Pro. In addition, you can also export the selected clips, selected sequences, and entire projects from Final Cut Pro in XML files. In Premiere Pro, a collection of clips and bins are maintained with specified names including various options in hierarchical order. Premiere Pro also allows you to retain the sequence markers, sequence settings, track layout, locked tracks, and sequence timecode start points of Final Cut Pro source project. Now let's learn to use the export settings dialog box.

Using the Export Settings Dialog Box

In Premiere Pro CS6, to access the Export Settings dialog box, you need to select File> Export> Media from the Menu bar. The Export Settings dialog box allows you to adjust the exporting settings for the required file format. In the next section, you explore formats to get an overview of the export options.

Exploring Formats to Export

In Premiere Pro, a video prepared with all the effects and adjustments applied can be exported in various other formats. Exporting to the required format helps you to play the video in different media, such as videotapes, still clips, Web, and Mobile devices. The Export Settings dialog box allows you to export in various formats using the Format option under the Export Settings group. The following are the formats available to export in Premiere Pro CS6:

- **Audio Interchange File Format:** Refers to an audio file format standard that is used for storing sound data for personal and other electronic audio devices. This format was developed by Apple computer in 1988, and is widely used on Apple Macintosh computer systems.
- **Microsoft AVI:** Refers to an **Audio Video Interleave**, known as AVI format. It is a multimedia container format developed by Microsoft in 1992. Microsoft AVI files can cover both audio and video data in a file that allows synchronous audio with video playback.
- **Windows Bitmap:** Refers to a file format used to store data of digital images. The term bitmap refers to a map of bits, synthetic or photographic. Raster images in general are referred to as bitmap images, as these files have an array of pixels.
- **DPX:** Refers to **Digital Picture Exchange** format used for digital intermediate and visual effect works. DPX format is worldwide chosen for still frames storage in most digital intermediate post productions. DPX is a file format suitable for almost any raster digital imaging applications. In addition, DPX formats provide a great deal of flexibility in storing color information, color spaces and color planes for exchange between production facilities. You can also allow for a wide variety of metadata to further clarify information stored (and storable) within each file.
- **Animated GIF:** Refers to an animated **Graphical Interchange Format**. This type of format is suited for solid-color motion graphics at a small frame size, such as animated company logo. It works better for synthetic graphics than for live-action video. It is convenient, because it is viewable in most Web browsers without requiring a plug-in, but you cannot include audio in an

animated GIF file. Export animated GIF like any other file, ensuring that you choose Animated GIF as the File Type. For best results, completed Animated GIF files should be tested in a Web browser before distributing.

- **GIF:** Refers to Graphical Interchange Format (GIF), which supports World Wide Web and gives maximum portability for the usage of bitmap images. This format supports up to 8 bits per pixel that allows a single image to reference a palette of up to 256 distinct colors. You can also achieve animations and can support separate palette of 256 colors for individual frame. This format is well suited for logos and graphics with rich solid colors.
- **JPEG:** Refers to Joint Photographic Experts Group (JPEG) which is commonly used as a compression format for photographic images. You can adjust the degree of compression by allowing a selectable range between storage size and image quality. You can compress various file formats in JPEG format. In addition, this file format is common image format that is used in digital camera and other capturing devices. This format is also commonly used for storing and transmitting photographic images on the World Wide Web.
- **MP3:** Refers to a format that creates audio files which are compatible with a wide variety of playback devices. MPEG (**Moving Picture Experts Group**)-1 or MPEG-2 audio layer 3 collectively gives a MP3 format intended for audio compression. This file format is commonly used for digital audio compression for the transfer and playback of music on digital audio players. These format files can be played using a player like Winamp, MusicMatch or Windows Media Player.
- **P2 Movie:** Refers to **Professional Plug-In** as a digital media storage format. This format helps you to feature tapeless (non-linear) recording of DV, DVCPRO, DVCPRO25, DVCPRO50, DVCPRO-HD, or AVC-Intra streams on a solid-state flash memory. You can also use this format in data transferring in a P2 card, which is basically a RAID of SD memory cards tightly packaged in a die-cast PC Card with an LSI controller and act as a memory capacity increases. In addition, you can also use these cards directly where a PC card slot is available, such as in notebook computers or in normal hard disk drives.
- **PNG:** Refers to **Portable Network Graphics** format that supports bitmapped images and serves lossless data compression. The PNG format supports palette-based images, grayscale images, and RGB images. PNG format was generated to improve upon and replace GIF (Graphics Interchange Format) as an image-file format not requiring an obvious authorization. The PNG format was designed for transferring images on the Internet.
- **Targa:** Refers to a file format used for describing bitmap images and is compatible for representing bitmaps from black and white, indexed color, and RGB color. This format also supports various compression methods that help scanners and imaging software for developing quality output. To be precise, this file format contains two leading parts, such as a header and a minimal header. The header indicates the color pixel information and the minimal header indicates the size of the bitmap as well as the amount of color information that the file contains.
- **TIFF:** Refers to **Tagged Image File Format** used for storing images. This image file format is widespread among graphical, publishing, and photographic industries. In addition, various other applications, such as scanning, word processing, character recognition, and faxing is supported by this format.
- **Windows Waveform:** Refers to a file format that manages sound devices over Waveform audio. There are two types of such devices: input device used for recording, and output device used for playing sounds. You can treat these devices independently for recording and playing individually. Every device is represented by a special handle, of the type HWAVEOUT for the output device and HWAVEIN for the input device. The variable of these types are used to indentify sound devices.

- **Audio Only:** Refers to an audio delivering format used for quality audio delivering purpose. Audio alone can be captured and optimized other than the video and presented in an audio module. In any sound track, the narrator explains and conveys the informational part of the video. For this, the audio module of the video must be presented in a qualified format. The audio can be captured and optimized fairly and it compresses well. You can also record low-frequency background noises, such as the hum of ventilation system.
- **FLV/F4V:** Refers to a Flash Video format that is published for playing in Flash players. This file format can exchange audio, video, and data over RTMP (Real Time Messaging Protocol) connections. The Flash player intuitively supports SWF files and also an FLV file, as the FLV files encode corresponding to audio and video streams. The audio and video data within the FLV files are encoded as audio and video within SWF files. These file formats can be played in Web and Mobile devices. In addition, you can also play the FLV and F4V format files in HD videos in mobile devices.
- **H.264:** Refers to a next-generation video compression technology in the MPEG-4 standard. This format files deliver excellent video quality across the entire bandwidth spectrum – from 3G to HD and everything in between (from 40 Kbps to upwards of 10 Mbps). This format is mostly used in recording, compressing, and distributing a standard of high quality definition video.
- **H.264 Blu-ray:** Refers to a file format used for video compression and is currently one of the most commonly used formats for recording, compression, and distribution of high definition video. You can make your H.264 for Blu-ray Disc settings, either by modifying an existing setting or creating a new setting in the Settings tab. The H.264 is perhaps best known as being one of the codec standards for Blu-ray Discs, as all the Blu-ray players must be able to decode H.264. This file format is supportive for streaming applications over the Web, such as playing video from YouTube and real time video conferencing.
- **MPEG4:** Refers to **Movie Picture Experts Group 4** (MPEG4) that defines compression of audio and visual digital data. This file format is used for Web (streaming media), voice (telephone, videophone), and broadcast television applications. MPEG-4 is a video standard defined by the Moving Picture Experts Group (MPEG). MPEG-4 file format was developed by Moving Picture Expert Group to stream multimedia video and audio at lower data rates and smaller file size. In addition, the MPEG-4 file format has the same algorithm of compression that MPEG-1 and MPEG-2 with including low bitrate encoding and 3D content, text and other media types. This file format has sustained a great impact in multimedia, graphics, and digital television applications.
- **Windows Media:** Refers to Windows Media Video format that supports video compression for several registered codec developed by Microsoft. The original video format, known as WMV, was originally designed for Internet streaming applications, as a competitor to Real Video. In addition, this file format contributes to provide physical transfer of formats, such as HD DVD and Blu-ray Disc from the WMV file format. This feature of Windows Media Video format as enabled through the Society of Motion Picture and Television Engineers (SMPTE).

Note: - Premiere Pro CS6 consists of various file formats such as MXF, MOV, AVI, FLV, and F4V that helps you to represent container file formats. On the other hand, you can denote the file formats on the basis of specific audio, video, or image. The container files can be defined as a file consisting of data that is encoded by means of various compressions and encoding schemes. For this, several codec must be installed into the operating system of your machine and work as a component inside the QuickTime or Video for Windows formats.

Exploring Export Options

In Premiere Pro, the Export Settings dialog box provides various options that help to adjust the export settings. There are several file formats, which will describe the output. It provides various presets of formats. You need to select the format best suited for your output objective. Let's learn more about the options present in the Export Settings dialog box in the following points:

- **Match Sequence Settings:** Allows you to match the sequence settings and apply to the whole sequence. The sequence settings done cannot be changed after a sequence is created.
- **Format:** Allows you to select from several file formats to export a video clip.
- **Preset:** Provides several predefined presets that you can select for exporting a video clip in Premiere Pro.
- **Comments:** Allows you to write or add comments to the video clips exporting to any location. You can mark the video with a text to remember the preparation details and anything related to the video clip.
- **Output Name:** Allows you to add name to the output video currently being exported.
- **Export Video:** Allows you to check it by giving allowance to export a video from the sequence to be exported.
- **Export Audio:** Allows you to check it by giving allowance to export the audio attached with the sequence to be exported.
- **Summary:** Displays the Output and Source video details, such as timing, quality, and speed.
- **Filters:** Allows you to add filter effects while exporting a clip, such as Gaussian Blur. This group also allows you to modify options related to the selected effect.
- **Use Maximum Render Quality:** Allows you to preserve detail when scaling from large formats to smaller formats or from high-definition to standard-definition formats. This feature maximizes the quality of motion in rendered clips and sequences. By selecting this check box, you can often render moving assets, such as animated clips sharply. This feature is opted only for the systems that have maximum quantity of RAM, as the rendering process needs the RAM memory. In addition, by maximizing rendering quality the image formats get highly compressed which results in artificial art effects due to sharpening of the colored pixels.
- **Use Previews:** Allows you to preview frames while rendering or exporting a video clip.
- **Use Frame Blending:** Allows you to smooth a clip that may appear jerky while applying an effect or transition on a video clip. The frame blending option operates only when there is a mismatch between sequence and clip frame rates. You can check the box and Premiere Pro application automatically averages the frames to create the necessary interpolated frames.
- **Queue:** Allows you to queue up the frames to be rendered for exporting the video clip in the specified export file format.
- **Export:** Allows you to export the modified settings to finalize and export a video clip.
- **Cancel:** Allows you to cancel the adjustments setting for exporting a video clip.
- **Source:** Displays the source video clip in the Monitor panel in the Export Settings dialog box of Premiere Pro screen.
- **Output:** Displays the output video clip in the Monitor panel in the Export Settings dialog box of Premiere Pro.
- **Source range:** Allows you to adjust the range from the source video clip. This feature has a ranging bar that consists of initial and finalized limit to be rendered for the output video clip. With this, we come to the end of export and export options. Let's now explore the project manger.

Lesson 15
Exploring the Project Manager
The functioning of the Project Manager commences when a project is completed. In Premiere Pro CS6, you can use the Project Manager to create a separate file folder that combines all the assets used in a sequence. You can easily archive a project and make it easier to access later when required. You can also conserve hard disk space by saving the specified assets that you want to use in the current project. Perform the following steps to open the Project Manager:

1. **Open** an existing project in Premiere Pro CS6. In our case, we open the project **New Project** containing **Sequence 01**, **Sequence 02**, and **Sequence 03**.

2. Choose **Project> Project Manager** from the Menu bar. First, it opens the Calculate Progress message box. Then, it opens the Project Manager dialog box on the screen. You are already familiarized with the Project Manager, so let's further learn about export sequence, nested sequence, and still images.

Exporting Sequence, Nested Sequences, and Still Images
After assembling and editing clips in sequence, you can generate the final video. The options you choose while producing the final video depends on its usage. To create a motion-picture film from an Adobe Premiere Pro project, you must have proper hardware for video or film transfer. Else, you should have access to a service provider that offers the appropriate equipment and services. The process of inserting a sequence into another sequence is known as nesting sequence. This process allows you to get a single linked video/audio clip though its source sequence may contain numerous video and audio tracks. In nested sequences or clips, you can select, move, trim, and apply effects. If you make any change to the source sequence, they are reflected in any nested instances created from it. You can create a complex group and hierarchy with nested sequences. In addition, Adobe Premiere Pro CS6 allows you to export frames or still image clips to a still image file. The frame is exported from the CTI position in the Timeline panel. In this section, you learn to export a sequence, nested sequence, and still image.

Exporting Sequence
In Premiere Pro CS6, you can export a sequence from the Timeline panel in any video file format. Exporting a sequence helps you to preview your work with effects, transitions, and adjustments applied on it. The sequences with less effects and slight modification requires less time as compared to the video with numerous effects and modifications done. Perform the following steps to export a sequence:

1. **Create** a new project in Premiere Pro CS6. Then **import** the desired video file in the Timeline panel. In our case, we import **Wildlife.wmv** video file.

2. Choose **File> Export> Media** from the Menu bar. It opens the Export Settings dialog box on the screen.

3. Enable (put check mark) the **Match Sequence Settings** check box under the Export Settings group. Then enable the **Use Maximum Render Quality** check box in the Export Settings dialog box.

4. Click the **Export** button in the Export Settings dialog box. It opens the **Encoding Sequence 01** dialog box which saves your sequence as **.avi** movie file. You can open this movie file in any media player.

Exporting Nested Sequences

Sequences cannot be nested within themselves. As nested sequences contain references to many clips, any action requires additional processing time. A current state of the source is reflected in a nested sequence. You can export a collection of sequences by nesting them. Thus, the distinct video clips in separate sequences can be exported in a video file format. The duration will be directly affected, as nested sequences contain a collection of sequences within them. The first duration of a nested sequence clip is set by its source. Perform the following steps to export nested sequences:

1. **Create** a new project in Premiere Pro CS6. In our case, we create the project named **Exporting Nested Sequence, Sequence 01**.

2. **Import** the desired video file in the Timeline panel. In our case, we import **Wildlife.wmv** video file in **Sequence 01**.

3. **Import** one more video file in the Timeline panel. In our case, we import **LightEffect.avi** video file in **Sequence 02**.

4. **Create** a new sequence named **Sequence 03** (as already explained in picture 1.2). Then **select** the Sequence 03 from the Timeline panel.

5. Drag and drop **LightEffect.avi** movie clip of Sequence 01 from the Project panel to the Timeline panel. Then drag and drop **Wildlife.wmv** movie clip of Sequence 02 from the Project panel to the Timeline panel.

6. Choose **File> Export> Media** from the Menu bar. It opens the Export Settings dialog box on the screen.

7. Enable the **Use Maximum Render Quality** check box. Then enable the **Use Preview** check box in the Export Settings dialog box.

8. Click the **Export** button in the Export Settings dialog box. It opens the **Encoding Sequence 03** dialog box which saves your sequence.

Exporting Still Images

In Premiere Pro CS6, you can export a clip of a frame as a still image. The specified frame can be exported in any still image formats. This can be useful to move a clip to animation and three-dimensional applications that do not import video file formats, or animation programs that requires a still-image. When you export a still image, Adobe Premiere Pro numbers the files automatically in versions of still image clips. Perform the following steps on your computer to export the video clip by using frames:

1. **Create** a new project in Premiere Pro CS6. Then **import** the desired video file in the Timeline panel. In our case, we import **Wildlife.wmv** video file.

2. **Select** the location of the **Current-Time Indicator** from the video clip where you want to add the first keyframe.

3. In the <u>Source Monitor</u> (or Program Monitor panel), click the **Export Frame** button, as shown in picture 3.6 with the red arrow. It opens the <u>Export Frame</u> dialog box on the screen.

4. **Type** a name for the still image in the <u>Name</u> text box. In our case, we retain the default name Sequene 01.Still001.

5. Click the down arrow beside the **Format** option under the Export Frame dialog box. It opens a dropdown list on the screen.

Picture 3.6

6. **Select** a format from the list in which you want to export the selected clip from the video. In our case, we select the **JPEG** format option.

7. Click the **OK** button to close the Export Frame dialog box. As the result, the selected frame from the Timeline panel is exported in a **JPEG** format.

Exporting Video for Web and Mobile Devices

In Premiere Pro CS6, you can export an organized video into any format that can be played in Web and Mobile devices. For playing video in Web and Mobile devices, you have to select a supporting format. You can export the video clip in the FLV and F4V formats, that allows you to play in Web and Mobile devices, as these formats are supported by the Flash player. By selecting the required exporting format, you can export a video sequence for use in Apple iPods, 3GPP cell phones, Sony PSPs, or other mobile devices. In Premiere Pro CS6, the Export Settings dialog box helps you to select an H.264 format preset made for the target device. Premiere Pro CS6 allows you to select from various predefined export settings options, which will helps to locate the best combination of file size and quality of audio and video to achieve the desired result. In this way, the files can be exported directly from the FLV and F4V formats. In Premiere Pro CS6, you can add the animation to add titles or other video sources. In addition, animations can be exported as an FLV or F4V format and further imported the application for modification. Perform the following steps to export video for Web and mobile devices:

1. **Create** a new project in Premiere Pro CS6. Then **import** the desired video file in the Timeline panel. In our case, we import **LightEffect.avi** video file.

2. Choose **File> Export> Media** from the Menu bar. It opens the <u>Export Settings</u> dialog box on the screen.

3. Click the down arrow button beside the **Format** option under the <u>Export Settings</u> group. Then select the **FLV|F4V** option from the open list.

4. Click the down arrow beside the **Preset** option under the <u>Export Settings</u> group. Then select the **FLV-Web Large, PAL Source (Flash 8 and Higher)** option from the list.

5. Enable the **Use Maximum Render Quality** check box. Then enable the **Use Preview** check box in the Export Settings dialog box.

6. Click the **Export** button in the Export Settings dialog box. It opens the **Encoding Sequence 01** dialog box which saves your sequence. With this, we come to the end of this chapter.

Niranjan Jha Showman
Trainer, Author, Physician, Entrepreneur, Filmmaker, Activist
Cromosys Corporation
Education and Technology Research Center
www.facebook.com/cromosys
+91-9561450045
Nallasopara (W), Mumbai, India

NIRANJAN JHA SHOWMAN

Founder - Niranjan Jha Showman

Education and Technology Research Center

Patankar Park, Nallasopara (W), Mumbai. +91-9561450045

Education, Technology, Publication, Healthcare, Newsmedia, Realtor, Filmmaking

www.facebook.com/cromosys

Cromosys Publication

Teach
Yourself
German

NIRANJAN JHA SHOWMAN

Cromosys Publication
Teach Yourself French
NIRANJAN JHA SHOWMAN

Cromosys Publication

Teach
Yourself
Spanish

NIRANJAN JHA SHOWMAN

Cromosys Publication

English Voice Accent and Pronunciation

NIRANJAN JHA SHOWMAN

Teach
Yourself
Autodesk
MAYA
Cromosys Publication
NIRANJAN JHA SHOWMAN

Cromosys Publication
Teach
Yourself
Autodesk
3ds Max
NIRANJAN JHA SHOWMAN

Cromosys Publication
CRIMINAL FACTORY
NIRANJAN JHA SHOWMAN

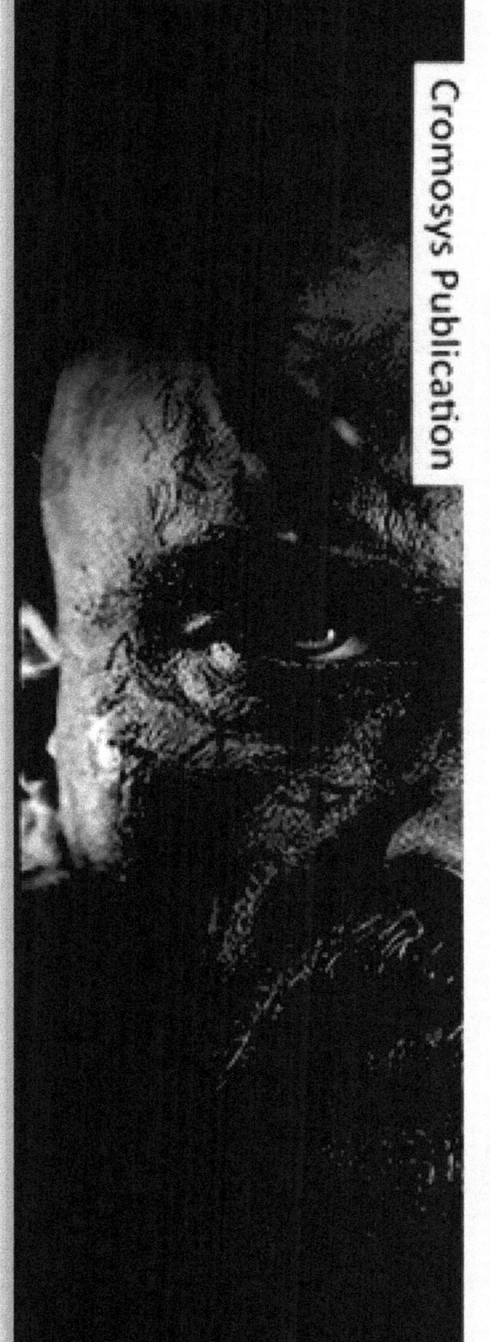

Cromosys Publication
FOCAL DISASTER
NIRANJAN JHA SHOWMAN

Cromosys Publication
Your talents will not help you succeed
without your skill of using them.
NIRANJAN JHA SHOWMAN
BE
MILLIONAIRE
LIKE
ME

Copyright Office
Government of India

सत्यमेव जयते

Extracts from the Register of Copyrights

Dated : 16/08/2022

1.	Registration Number	: **T-88782-2022**
2.	Name, address and nationality of the applicant	: NIRANJAN JHA SHOWMAN, CROMOSYS PUBLICATION, 001, JAYSATYAM, PATANKAR ROAD, NALLASOPARA (W), MUMBAI, MAHARASHTRA - 401203. INDIAN
3.	Nature of the applicant's interest in the copyright of the work	: AUTHOR
4.	Class and description of the work	: LITERARY / BOOK
5.	Title of the work	: **Teach Yourself Adobe Premiere Pro**
6.	Language of the work	: ENGLISH
7.	Name, address and nationality of the author and if the author is deceased, date of his decease	: NIRANJAN JHA SHOWMAN, CROMOSYS PUBLICATION, 001, JAYSATYAM, PATANKAR ROAD, NALLASOPARA (W), MUMBAI, MAHARASHTRA - 401203. INDIAN
8.	Whether the work is published or unpublished	: UNPUBLISHED
9.	Year and country of first publication and name, address and nationality of the publisher	: N.A.
10.	Years and countries of subsequent publications, if any, and names, addresses and nationalities of the publishers	: N.A. SAME AS ABOVE
11.	Names, addresses and nationalities of the owners of various rights comprising the copyright in the work and the extent of rights held by each, together with particulars of assignments and licences, if any	:
12.	Names, addresses and nationalities of other persons, if any, authorised to assign or licence of rights comprising the copyright	: N.A.
13.	If the work is an 'Artistic work', the location of the original work, including name, address and nationality of the person in possession of the work. (In the case of an architectural work, the year of completion of the work should also be shown).	: N.A.
14.	If the work is an 'Artistic work', whether it is registered under the Designs Act 2000 if yes give details.	: N.A.
15.	If the work is an 'Artistic work', capable of being registered as a design under the Designs Act 2000.whether it has been applied to an article though an industrial process and ,if yes ,the number of times it is reproduced.	: N.A.
16.	Remarks, if any	:

Diary Number :   8623/2020-DF/T
Date of Application :   25/07/2020
Date of Receipt :   25/07/2020

DEPUTY REGISTRAR OF COPYRIGHTS

Cromosys Publication

Teach Yourself Adobe Premiere Pro

NIRANJAN JHA SHOWMAN